CULTURE SHOCK!
Denmark

Morten Strange

Graphic Arts Center Publishing Company
Portland, Oregon

In the same series

Argentina	Ecuador	Laos	Sri Lanka
Australia	Egypt	Malaysia	Sweden
Austria	Finland	Mauritius	Switzerland
Belgium	France	Mexico	Syria
Bolivia	Germany	Morocco	Taiwan
Borneo	Greece	Myanmar	Thailand
Brazil	Hong Kong	Nepal	Turkey
Britain	Hungary	Netherlands	UAE
California	India	Norway	Ukraine
Canada	Indonesia	Pakistan	USA
Chile	Iran	Philippines	USA—The South
China	Ireland	Saudi Arabia	Venezuela
Costa Rica	Israel	Scotland	Vietnam
Cuba	Italy	Singapore	
Czech Republic	Japan	South Africa	
Denmark	Korea	Spain	

Barcelona At Your Door	Paris At Your Door	A Student's Guide
Beijing At Your Door	Rome At Your Door	A Traveller's Medical
Chicago At Your Door	San Francisco At Your	Guide
Havana At Your Door	Door	A Wife's Guide
Jakarta At Your Door	Shanghai At Your Door	Living and Working
Kuala Lumpur, Malaysia	Tokyo At Your Door	Abroad
At Your Door	Vancouver At Your Door	Personal Protection At
London At Your Door		Home & Abroad
Moscow At Your Door	A Globe-Trotter's Guide	Working Holidays
Munich At Your Door	A Parent's Guide	Abroad
New York At Your Door		

Illustrations by TRIGG
Photographs by the author unless otherwise stated

© 1996 Times Editions Pte Ltd
© 2000 Times Media Private Limited
Revised 2000, 2003
Reprinted 1997, 1998, 1999, 2001, 2003

This book is published by special
arrangement with Times Media Private Limited
Times Centre, 1 New Industrial Road, Singapore 536196
International Standard Book Number 1-55868-762-9
Library of Congress Catalog Number 96-075616
Graphic Arts Center Publishing Company
P.O. Box 10306 • Portland, Oregon 97296-0306 • (503) 226-2402

Printed in Singapore

To Adam, Daniel and Simon
May Denmark be good to you.

CONTENTS

PREFACE

I was born in Denmark, I was raised there, I went to school there. And yet when I grew up I didn't feel that Denmark offered me the opportunities I was seeking. So at 20 years of age I went abroad to work. I was 40 when I moved back.

By then I had spent almost all my adult life abroad. I had to start in Denmark from scratch, setting up a home, a business, a career and a social life in a culture in many ways alien to what I had become used to. I had the advantage though, that unlike most other strangers, I spoke the language – although not always quite as fluently as a native.

I have met many foreigners who love Denmark, who come back here year after year to visit Copenhagen and to walk on the wide, open beaches of Jutland. The people are so friendly they say, the landscape is so pretty and neat. But I know for a fact that not all outsiders feel that way, many have difficulties coping with Danish society and some end up in conflict with their peers and with the authorities, the ultimate case of culture shock.

It has been said that the Danes are not a nation, they are a tribe and there is some truth in that. Like all tribes they have a culture of their own, a set of norms and rules and regulations, different from all others. Some norms are written down and can easily be explained but others are more hazy, they make up a protocol of expectations and behaviour not obviously understood by somebody from another culture. So the foreigner, on top of the practical difficulties of travelling and settling in a new country, has to deal with a cultural transformation and inevitably some degree of culture shock.

This book covers most aspects of Danish life, some of it is strictly factual, some is based on personal experiences. I have tried to distinguish quite clearly between the two.

It is my hope that by sharing some of my experiences and a bit of general knowledge of the country with other newcomers I can help to make their stay in Denmark enjoyable and successful

ACKNOWLEDGEMENTS

For making this book possible I would like to thank Simon Kolbe Strange and Daniel Kolbe Strange, they are both seven-years-old and my sons and I wouldn't have done this without them, and also Adam Kolbe Strange who is a wonderful three-year-old and also my son, born on the darkest day of the year but the sunshine of my life.

I thank my relatives in Denmark and Norway, especially my mother, former member of parliament Ebba Strange, whose great humanitarian ideals I cannot always agree with but always sympathise with and respect.

I thank my hard working former colleagues and fellow volunteers at the Danish Ornithological Society, DOF/Bird Life-Denmark, especially Director Arne Jensen, who believed in me when I started out as an employee. And I thank all my associates within the Bird Life Internationale Secretariat in Cambridge who have enabled me to maintain an international perspective on things.

I would like to thank the many friends I have in Asia, especially Dr Hans-Ulrich Bernard, Dr Clive Briffett, Dr Chua Ee Chiam, Iain Ewing, Allen Jeyarajasingam, Aileen Lau, Lim Kim Keang, Lim Kim Seng, Ng Bee Choo, Dr Wim Verheught and many others.

For helping me with photographs for this book I would especially like to express my gratitude to Jens Henriksen and Lone Eg Nissen for the use of photographs.

Finally I would like to thank my good neighbours at Milepælen, Skødstrup near Århus for being that – good neighbours, especially Jens Erik Rasmussen and Peder Falk, who came to my rescue when my old AT 286 started acting up just as I was about to complete this book!

Author's notes on this book

I have used the conventional spelling for places known worldwide, like Copenhagen and Greenland and also three other major parts of the country, Jutland, Funen and Zealand. The rest of the localities do not have international names and the Danish ones have been used.

Figures in the book are valid as of January 2003. Politics and economics change, but people change very slowly. Denmark as a nation is more than 1,000-years-old. Some of the cultural characteristics described here might endure for another 1,000 years.

Chapter One

INTRODUCING DENMARK

GETTING TO KNOW THE PLACE

Whatever your expectations of Denmark were before arriving, you are bound to be in for a few surprises once you get there. The Danish society is not an easy one to penetrate. On the surface it appears to function well, the infrastructure is all in place, the people usually speak English and are easy to approach. But if you spend more than a few days in the country you will find that this nation operates at a number of levels. Chit-chatting with new people you meet is easy. But integrating deeper into society and establishing yourself with a network of local friends is a lot harder – people in Denmark appear to already have all the friends they need, or so many foreigners comment.

The Danes have traditionally formed a very homogeneous society with well established rules and unwritten codes of conduct. It is a very free society – you are free to conform. But as a foreigner you do not behave like everybody else, sometimes you do things differently. Certainly your background, your experiences, your expectations set you apart. So be prepared for some situations where you will surprise or offend people, or perhaps they will offend you. In other words, prepare yourself for culture shock.

Added to this is the fact that conditions are changing rapidly these days in Denmark. The Danish people currently find themselves in an identity crisis, and their relationship with the nations around them is at the centre of it. As a foreigner you have an important part to play, even if you try to stay neutral. For instance, the Danes are grappling with their status within the European Union; an independent country with a history that goes back more than a thousand years is in the process of relinquishing sovereignty in an unprecedented way. On top of that, the welfare system that the Danes have so proudly pioneered and which represents the backbone of the Danish sense of security is under pressure and there is uncertainty over what to do about it. The influx of foreigners attracted by the system plays a part in all this, so again the problem links up to international relations. These issues are charged with emotion for the Danes and they split the society down the middle in endless discussions and confrontations.

Getting to know a country is a lengthy process, like peeling an onion – every time you remove one layer another one turns up. It is an exciting process that never really seems to end, you slowly work your way towards the core but you never quite get there. In all walks of life knowledge is a good ballast, knowledge and skills always command respect and they help build your confidence and your enthusiasm. People like people who are confident and enthusiastic and in a new country knowledge will provide you with a cushion against those periodic cases of culture shock. So at this stage, a bit of general knowledge of the land is a good place to start.

A COUNTRY OF ISLANDS

Denmark is a small country, so its inhabitants frequently will remind you, but don't let this apparent modesty fool you. What the Danes really mean when they say this is, "We are just a small country but we have done very well for ourselves." This is quite true, up to a certain extent.

The total land area of Denmark covers 43,100 square kilometres. The Jutland Peninsula is connected to the European mainland and shares a border with Germany to the south. Slightly less than half of the Danish population lives on Jutland. The rest of the country consists of islands – all 406 of them. Of these islands 76 are inhabited but only 17 have more than 1,000 residents.

The largest island is Zealand where the capital Copenhagen is located, facing Sweden. Almost two million people live on Zealand and another 150,000 nearby on Amager Island where the International Airport of Copenhagen is located at Kastrup. Funen is located between Jutland and Zealand and to many Danes the island is just that – a transit area that you have to cross when you travel from Zealand across to Jutland and the European continent or vice versa, nevertheless 433,000 people call this island home.

The most remote of the islands is Bornholm, in the Baltic Sea, between Sweden and Poland. Denmark almost lost this island in 1945 after the Second World War when Soviet forces occupied it while the rest of Denmark was liberated from German occupation by British troops. However, the Russians decided to withdraw again, making Bornholm one of the only territories that they pulled out of voluntarily after the war.

Most of the small inhabited islands are located in the archipelagos south of Funen and Zealand and many just cover a few square kilometres, some less than one. On Tornø, Romsø, Ejlinge and Hesselø there are only two registered inhabitants, on Store Svelmø and Ejlinge there are just half that!

THE SEA IN BETWEEN

As you can imagine, with this kind of geography the sea is almost as important to the Danes as the land. The fact that you have to cross one every time you arrive at or leave the capital island is a telling reminder of this. Travelling on ferries is something Danes do all the time and most people live within a few kilometres of the coast. Summer or winter, people go to the local beach or harbour for relaxation and recreation. Practically everybody knows how to swim and swimming lessons are part of the compulsory curriculum in state schools. The sea breeze permeates the air everywhere, with that characteristic sensation of cool, salty moisture.

Although car ferries remain an important mode of transport, nowadays many of the islands are connected with bridges and between Jutland and Funen there are two of them. A huge multi-billion dollar scheme to connect Funen and Zealand will be completed in 1997 for trains and 1998 for cars – three years behind schedule and one hundred percent above budget but nevertheless a major infrastructural improvement to the country. This project is one of the biggest of its kind worldwide currently in progress and the biggest ever undertaken in Denmark. The fixed connection across Storebælt, as this 18 kilometre wide strait is called, will consist of a bridge, a tunnel drilled under the sea-bed for trains and a bridge all the way for cars, but bicycles will not be allowed access.

In 2000 the landmasses of Sweden and Denmark were again connected in another historic project. The 16 km.-long Øresunds Connection is a tunnel and bridge for both cars and trains (again no pedestrians or bicycles). The starting point is just south of Copenhagen near Kastrup Airport. At the opening ceremony, on 1 July 2000, Queen Margrethe II and King Carl Gustav XVI of Sweden, their spouses, plus the respective PMs met on the middle of the bridge in a moving ceremony, which was televised worldwide and watched by an estimated 800 million viewers. Check out www.oeresundsbron.com for current crossing information, live webcam views etc.

The Danish coastline is very varied, with narrow, sandy beaches usually facing east and muddy estuaries near rivers and around the Wadden Sea in the southwestern part of Jutland. Fiords and inlets are often surrounded by picturesque salt marshes and pastures. Especially spectacular is the west coast of Jutland which has miles and miles of wide-open sandy beaches and large sand dunes just behind. Residents and tourists alike flock to the Danish coasts to sail on the waters and to hunt, bird watch or just hike around or picnic nearby - some even swim in the sea which at any time of the year is absolutely freezing cold.

PHYSICAL FEATURES

Himmelbjerget, is a pretty hill in the middle of Jutland which rises sharply from a lake nearby, has a tower at the top and is usually packed with day-trippers during the summer months. Himmelbjerget actually means 'the sky mountain,' a fairly ambitious name for a hill 147 metres high! Three other Danish hills are actually higher, with Yding Skovhøj at 173 metres the highest. Gudenåen (meaning God Creek) running nearby Himmelbjerget is, at 158 kilometres, the longest stream in the country. By common convention Denmark doesn't have any waters befitting the term river although Gudenåen definitely looks like one in many places. It is a wonderful place to go canoeing or sailing in the summer. There are about 1,000 named lakes in Denmark, six cover more than 10 square kilometres, the largest is Arresø at 39.5 square kilometres.

When you travel across Denmark it appears quite built up. In spite of that, all the developed areas including towns, villages, farms and roads only constitute 12% of the country's surface. No less than 76% is actually cultivated fields and fragmented patches of wilder landscapes including moors, marshes, sand dunes and lakes.

The remaining 12% is forest, in other words Denmark has a forest cover equal to Thailand and many other countries associated with teeming wildlife. A political decision has been made to double this

coverage to 25% within this century. But the forest in Denmark is not primary vegetation in its original state. The widespread forests of mainly oak trees that used to cover the land have been cut long ago – much of the felling was done 300–400 years ago to build warships during a military build up and general spur of development at that time. The forests today are all managed plantations of mostly spruce, pine and other softwood coniferous trees, with some deciduous park-like forests of mainly tall, hardwood beech trees and oaks. Only a small percentage of the forest cover is mixed woodlands but these forests are much richer in birds and mammals than the pretty but slightly sterile monoculture plantations.

WILDLIFE

Most large animals disappeared from Denmark when agriculture became established over 2,000 years ago. Bear, lynx and wolverine vanished around that time, as did moose, although the occasional animal has turned up in forests in North Zealand, probably crossing the sea of ice from Sweden during severe winters. Wolf hung on until the early 18th century when the last animal was shot out. There are rumours that wolf populations are today spreading west from Eastern

15

Europe into northern Germany so the wolf may yet re-establish itself in Denmark. The wild boar is well on its way to doing so, partly from escaped captive animals and partly from natural expansion into Jutland from Germany.

Today the largest animal in Denmark is the elk, a large member of the deer family, with some healthy wild populations, especially in western Jutland. The roe deer is another native animal that is holding on in spite of hunting pressure. With expanding forest cover it is doing quite well and it is the most common deer in the country and you may be lucky enough to spot one if you go for a quiet walk near some remote forest clearing.

There are 54 species of mammals living in Denmark, most are bats and small rodents. Many mammals are rare and nocturnal and are not easy to see. Even the red squirrel is not common these days. I have spent a lot of time at natural sites but I have never seen a badger nor an otter or a marten, which are all supposed to be there. The fox is doing better and will come into built up areas and residential estates. Hares are common and you often see one running across the fields as you drive through the country. The porcupine is a delightful little animal that you can attract into your garden by putting out food for it.

There are few reptiles in this cold climate, although I have on occasions seen the only Danish poisonous snake, the adder sunning itself on some remote trail. There are 177 resident birds and a total of 412 species have been recorded, including migratory birds. I can recommend becoming involved with one of the local nature watching societies, it is a pleasant way of getting to know the Danish country, its wildlife and its people.

THE DANES

A total of 5,275,121 people lived in Denmark as of 2002. In the last few years about 65,000 babies have been added to the population annually. For a period in the 1980s the natural population increase was negative, which means that more people were dying than being born. Denmark had one of the lowest birthrates in Europe and the world at this time but today it is about average for Europe and higher than many southern European and predominantly Catholic nations like Italy and Spain.

You may get the impression when you arrive in Denmark that a large number of the people are old. This is partly because the low birthrate for many years has in fact generated a large proportion of elderly in the society and partly because old people in Denmark remain active, have money, and tend to go out travelling, shopping and socialising.

When there is a small population increase in a given year it is usually because immigration exceeds emigration. Each year more people settle in Denmark than leave. In 2001, the figure was 17,079.

THE WEATHER AND THE SEASONS

Denmark is located at 56th northern latitude. On the other side of the Atlantic Ocean this is equivalent to Labrador, Canada where huge icebergs are floating in the sea or the panhandle of Alaska facing the Pacific Ocean with its massive glaciers of permanent ice formations. It is cold in Denmark – but not quite that bad. This is because of some warm sea currents from the Caribbean that are being pushed north and east across the Atlantic towards northern Europe and which keep coastal winter temperatures there rather high.

Consequently, Denmark has a typical coastal climate with generally mild winters, cool summers and precipitation spread out all through the year. The Danes will tell you that they have four seasons, but in actual fact they only have two – the summer when the weather is quite pleasant and the rest of the year when it is miserable!

They do however, divide the year into sections of three months and as you spend more time in the country you will learn to recognise some very subtle changes in conditions.

The Danish winter can certainly be a test of endurance as this picture shows but the Danes take it all in their stride.

The following figures are average numbers for 1961–1990, starting with spring, through to the daunting Danish winter:

Month	Temp. (°C)	Rainfall (mm)	Sunshine (Hrs)
Mar	2.1	46	114
Apr	5.7	41	179
May	10.8	48	246
Jun	14.3	55	233
Jul	15.6	66	236
Aug	15.7	67	220
Sep	12.7	73	145
Oct	9.1	76	97
Nov	4.7	79	58
Dec	1.6	66	36
Jan	0.0	57	39
Feb	0.0	38	69
All year	7.7	712	1,670

This is the official version. Actually it works such that in the first week of May the landscape transforms as all the deciduous trees and bushes turn green. People throw off their winter gear and store it away in the back of the closet. Suddenly you can see what people look like, the boys think that the girls look a lot prettier and maybe it works the other way too. In June/July life is a breeze, it may rain a bit but it is seldom really cold and never really hot. However there is always an element of unpredictability, a major topic of discussion amongst Danes each fall is how the summer was. Temperatures can drop below freezing in any month of the year – except in July where it has not been below 0°C in many years.

June 24 is the longest day of the year – the sun rises at 4:28 a.m. and doesn't set until 9:55 p.m. On a clear day it is virtually light all through the night this time of year and at daybreak the morning chorus of singing garden birds is a true delight.

Around the end of August it all comes to an end. For the foreigner this is when you might like to plan an excuse for visiting the old country or getting away to some other place. Apart from the occasional moment of clear, calm weather you are in for a long, bad spell here. In October the leaves wither and, after a short period of fantastic colours of reds and yellows across the forests, the landscape turns grey and bleak. December and January are definitely not good times to be above the 45th parallel. December 22 is the shortest day of the year in Denmark, with the sun rising at 8:40 a.m. and creeping along the horizon for a while before it sets shortly afterwards at 3:37 p.m. On rainy days it never seems to get really bright at all.

Those anticipating a season of skiing or ice-skating may be disappointed as all you get are some occasional blizzards that seem to take the country by surprise each year and paralyse the transport systems for a few days. Then it will thaw and rain and freeze intermittently again. This is when the Danes really show their character and you cannot help but admire them when, morning after morning, they venture out into the total darkness to scrape ice off the

In contrast to the winter landscape, a summer's day in the Danish countryside is mild and sunny. Although the season itself is short, the days are long due to Denmark's northern location. (Photo: Lone Eg Nissen)

windows of their cars and then drive along icy and deadly roads to get to work. It is dark again by the time they are off and return home.

You may stand some November day at your window and look at the people outside running through a hailstorm, seeking cover amongst the buildings, like civilians under sniper-fire in some war-torn city and you might wonder why humans ever travelled to this part of Europe in the first place. Well, they did, and they managed very well for a while too.

A BIT OF HISTORY

The Danish nation is an old civilization, with a long and complicated history. It contains many changes in rulers, wars, territorial expansions and contractions. Confronted with a test, few Danes would likely know all the details about previous kings and historic conditions, certainly this knowledge would not be expected of a foreigner. However, a brief rundown of the most important historic events might be useful.

200,000 B.C. – Some stone tools dating as far back as this have been found in Jutland.

11,000 B.C. – The beginning of the first continuous human habitation in Denmark. The last Ice Age was coming to an end at this time, global sea levels were still low, you could walk dry-footed from England across Denmark to Sweden – and some people did. The climate and landscape was sub-Arctic, the people hunted caribou and seals and drifted from camp to camp.

4,000 B.C. – The first appearance of agriculture and permanent settlements. Tools still made of stone. Sea levels and temperatures rise creating the present landscape of temperate forests and islands.

2,000 B.C. – Metal tools being introduced: copper, tin and bronze; the so-called Bronze Age.

500 B.C. – Tools and weapons of iron introduced. The people in Denmark travel and trade increasingly within Europe to the south.

A.D. **700** – Denmark starts functioning as a nation under one ruler.

A.D. **800** – The Viking era starts. For the next two hundred years people from Denmark and what is now Norway travel far in their long, wooden boats. (No, the Vikings did not wear horned helmets, they went out of fashion after the Bronze Age), but they did invade and settle in all of England, the Atlantic islands, large parts of France and what are now the Baltic states.

A.D. **960** – Christianity introduced. Harald Blåtand becomes the first Christian king.

1035 – King Knud the Great dies. His kingdom, which included England, Scotland and most of Scandinavia disintegrates.

1167 – Copenhagen is founded.

1185 – Denmark expands into parts of Germany.

1332 – Denmark ruined, creditors from Germany and Sweden hold power.

1348–50 – The 'Black Death' plague epidemic greatly reduces the population.

1360 – Valdemar Atterdag restores Danish rule.

1380 – Norway and Iceland are annexed by Denmark.

1397 – Queen Margrethe I establishes control over all of Scandinavia including Sweden.

1448–1523 – Sweden gains independence after much fighting.

1563–70 – War with Sweden.

1611–1613 – Another war with Sweden.

1625 – War with Germany, ends in defeat.

1643–45 – Yet another war with Sweden.

1657–60 – War with Sweden again, a final, crushing defeat. Denmark loses all Swedish territory, Denmark in ruins but the Danish king now rules parts of present day Germany plus Norway and Iceland.

1675–79 – War with Sweden.

1700–1721 – War with Sweden. Denmark finally gives up trying to regain former ground. (Is it any wonder that emotions run high even today when Denmark meets Sweden in a soccer friendly?)

1801 – Denmark joins the Napoleonic Wars – siding with the French which was obviously a bad move – Sweden joined in with England (the winning party) and after a number of naval defeats Denmark has to hand over Norway for Swedish rule in 1814.

1849 – Civil democracy is introduced, the first constitution is signed, allowing parliamentary rule.

1864 – War with Germany, ends in defeat. Denmark loses part of southern Jutland.

1914 – First World War, Denmark remains neutral.

1920 – After German defeat in Europe and a referendum in the area, Denmark is allowed to annex part of the area lost in 1864.

1940 – Second World War, Denmark tries to stay neutral but is occupied by Nazi Germany.

1944 – Invaded by American forces, Iceland breaks away from Denmark and becomes an independent republic. Denmark now has its present day borders.

1945 – Denmark liberated by Allied forces.

1949 – Denmark gives up neutrality and joins NATO.

1972 – Margrethe II, the present Danish sovereign, becomes queen.

1973 – Denmark joins the European Economic Community (EEC) through a referendum.

1993 – Another referendum allows Denmark to progress with the rest of the EEC into the European Union (EU) under the Maastricht Treaty.

1998 – Yet another referendum regarding EU membership chipping away at Danish sovereignty. The Amsterdam Treaty was approved by a majority of Danish voters, allowing for expansion of the EU, with new members from the Eastern European block.

2000 – Another EU-related referendum. This time Danish voters rejected further integration by voting NO to the common EU currency, the EURO by a 53/47 % margin.

THE NORDIC MYTHOLOGY

Denmark shares a certain affiliation with the other Nordic countries, not just by the repeated fighting with Sweden, but by an old culture which is shared. I have not gone into details about all the different kings and folk heroes that emerged through these developments and it doesn't seem very significant these days. There are some fascinating folk legends, however, and more information is available in the titles on Danish history mentioned at the back of this book.

The Viking era and the old Nordic cultures still loom large in the minds of many Danes today and form an important part of the national heritage and identity.

Before Christianity arrived, the Danes believed in a peculiar world of gods that are unique to the Nordic or at least northern European culture. Some present day Danish names and terms are derived from this mythology as well as names for places, persons and even weekdays. Odin was head of the gods, Thor was his son and an unrestrained warrior. Balder was another of Odin's sons, killed through tragic treason. The love-goddess Frej was there, and so was the sly Loke, who on occasions collaborated with the rival bad-guys, some coward demons who lived next door. This mythology has been retold by modern Danish writers complete with a terrifying apocalyptic ending and makes for great reading. The stories are free from the poorly disguised nationalistic agenda present in many other historic references, and are rich in universal human drama and symbolism.

DANISH COLONIES

Sometimes reference is made in the Danish media to former Danish colonies, often in travel stories with a bit of a nostalgic flavour. In reality, Denmark was never a great colonial power like some other European nations but they did venture out on a few occasions to get a piece of the action.

In Asia, Denmark had colonies at Tranquebar on the Indian east coast and at Serampore in what is now Bangladesh as well as the Nicobar Islands in the Indian Ocean. They were trading and missionary stations operating from 1660 until 1848, when they were sold to the British.

In Africa there were some Danish colonies and trading posts in what is now Ghana on the west coast of the continent. Starting in 1658 Denmark for a while controlled about 150 kilometres of the coastline before selling out to the British in 1850.

Most recently Denmark occupied some islands in the Caribbean – St. Thomas, St. Jan and St. Croix, east of Puerto Rico. This area is now called the Virgin Islands. There were some plantation operations there but as a whole the area didn't really benefit Denmark and was a money losing business. The islands were sold to the United States in 1917 and the colonial days of Denmark were over.

Greenland

Greenland and the Faroe Islands are still part of the Danish kingdom. They were annexed together with Norway in 1380 and have remained under Danish rule ever since. It is a local joke amongst Danish kids to ask the visitor, "Which country is the largest in Europe?" and while you suggest France or Germany the answer is of course Denmark. Including the 2,175,600 square kilometres of Greenland Denmark covers the largest area – now you have been warned!

Most of the interior of Greenland is of course covered by a permanent ice-shield and only 55,000 people live along the coast, most of them native Eskimos. Some people still live in remote villages and fish and hunt seals from small boats much like they have always done, but today most natives stay in modern communities although in many cases they are not doing well. Stories of social problems reach the Danish media periodically but in later years there are signs that the Greenlanders are coming to terms with modern life.

Greenland used to be a place where Danes travelled, mostly single males, to make a buck (tax free) in construction or industrialisation development projects. That was before 1978 when Greenland achieved a more autonomous status called 'Home Rule.' Income tax for guest workers was introduced and, among other things, Greenland opted

In Greenland, popular with Danish tourists, traditional transportation methods are still often the most effective means of getting around. (Photo: Jens Henriksen)

out of the EEC. Now most Danes go there for adventure tourism.

The Americans operate a huge DEW (Distant Early Warning) base at Thule in northeastern Greenland but the importance of this installation has diminished due to the end of the Cold War. Thule once in a while pops up in the Danish news with reference to an accident at the base a few years back – a B52 bomber carrying atomic warheads crashed near the airstrip spreading plutonium all over the snow. Danish workers who helped clean up the mess have been dying of cancer at unusually high rates since and their families are now suing the government for compensation.

Socially, Home Rule seems to have done Greenland good but full independence is not really on the cards. The island is too thinly populated to function as a nation and the economy remains weak. Danish financial support is increasing rather than decreasing every year and is currently at over 600 million dollars per year – around 12,000 dollars for every person on the island.

The Faroe Islands

The Faroe Islands consist of 18 small, windswept islands in the middle of the Atlantic Ocean inhabited by 43,000 people of the

Nordic race. They have a degree of home rule similar to Greenland's but national defence, most foreign affairs, the judiciary and parts of the economy are still Danish responsibility.

For a long period starting in the 1960s and lasting well into the 1980s the place was booming and people became prosperous from working with fishing and in fishing-related industries. Then the Faroe Islands turned into a classic example of overspending and poor planning. A combination of incompetence, corruption and a loss of industry has severely affected the economic stability of the islands.

Today economic life on the Faroe Islands is slowly recovering as fishing is improving. The debt, however, is still there and nobody knows exactly how large it is or what to do with it. The islands are about a billion and a half dollars short – 35,000 dollars per person.

In this book the description of Denmark refers to the southern parts only, excluding the North Atlantic autonomous regions.

A REMARKABLE TRANSFORMATION

In geological and historic terms Denmark and the rest of northern Europe have undergone a physical and social evolution that was rapid and revolutionary without comparison.

Although economic and political power bases shift around the world like drifting sand and at the moment seem to be moving out of western Europe, this is nevertheless where modern civilisation, technology and also some universal cultural values originated. It is useful to keep that in perspective on occasions.

And the evolutionary process hasn't stopped, although what is going to happen next no one of course can say for sure. But certainly the world is growing smaller in the sense that information is circulated quickly now, travel is easy and cheap, values are shared and new alliances are being formed all the time. The role of the national state is changing and international rather than national events now determine future developments. In Denmark the nation's place within the world community is this era's hot topic.

— Chapter Two —

THE DANES AND THEIR WORLD

ARRIVING

With Denmark becoming part of the European Union (EU) in 1994 you may have thought that entry procedures would become more relaxed – not so. In fact in March 1994 I arrived back from Asia and for the first time immigration officials had moved out from their booths on the ground floor of the Kastrup Airport and had positioned themselves right at the exit door of the plane, screening passengers before they could advance into the transit lounge.

There are many entry ports into Denmark. If you arrive from one of the other Scandinavian countries, by ferry from Norway or Sweden for example, Nordic nationals are not obliged to even show their passports and the atmosphere is generally less formal.

With the income taxes and car and property prices being significantly lower in Sweden these days some Danes have even settled in Malmö just across from Copenhagen. The 8 a.m. speed ferry to the city has come to look like some commuter train into New York or London, when all the working folk with their coats and ties and briefcases disembark for a day's work at the office. The sea journey to Norway of course is longer and is only done by vacationers.

There are several international airports in Denmark but by far the largest and the only one with transcontinental connections is Kastrup. This is where most immigrants and overseas visitors arrive and where immigration checks are most stringent.

Alternatively you can drive in or go by rail across the German border. If you go by rail you usually have to change trains at the Padborg station; few connections will take you directly across the border. There you pass through an immigration check on the platform. It is all fairly laid back, but naturally your papers must be *in ordnung* as the Germans say.

If you drive, you will notice that most people just hold up their passports to the windscreen and go through the checkpoint, which looks like a motorway toll gate. Customs are pretty much a formality these days.

There are some rules regarding the number of bottles of wine and beer you can bring into Denmark but the regulations change so frequently, as EU policies are further harmonised, that some customs officers at one time told the media that they honestly weren't sure what the rules were or how they should be interpreted. Very few cars are stopped and searched.

Just before the border are some incredible shopping malls where Danes pull in to save a few dollars by filling their trunks with canned beer. The staff at the stores all speak Danish. Danes used to also fill up with petrol here, but now it is cheaper in Denmark and Germans are the ones that go abroad to gas up.

WHO CAN STAY IN DENMARK?

If you are from another Nordic country you do not need permission to stay and work in Denmark. The five Nordic countries are Denmark, Norway, Sweden, Iceland and Finland. They maintain formal ties through the Nordic Council. The first three are the so called Scandinavian countries, their cultures are particularly closely linked and their languages are similar and can be understood throughout the region. After two years of residence you can apply for citizenship.

If you are from another EU country you must apply for permission to stay more than three months, but you have a right to stay in Denmark if there is a job for you, if you operate a business or if you are otherwise economically independent. After seven years you can apply for citizenship.

If you are from outside the EU you can visit Denmark for three months. If you are a citizen of any country in North or South America or Australia, New Zealand, Malaysia, Thailand, Korea and Japan you do not need a visa. A citizen from any other country in Asia and Africa must apply before going. For some selected countries, which have recently included Ghana, Ethiopia, Somalia, Afghanistan, Sri Lanka and Bosnia, a visa is usually refused. Check the Danish Foreign Ministry as this list of countries is revised yearly. If you want to stay longer than three months you must apply for permission. The law can grant you residence status if you are a student of if you have special skills needed by a Danish employer. However, few work permits are granted on merit. Since 1973 there has been a virtual stop on foreign workers in Denmark, even for skilled and qualified personnel.

There is no scheme allowing investors resident status. Many other countries offer wealthy and entrepreneurial individuals immigration priority but this does not happen in Denmark.

At the moment only two categories of non-EU foreigners are allowed residency. The first is a spouse, child below the age of 18 or parent above the age of 60 of a permanent resident and the second is a political refugee.

For residents to bring in their close families is of course fairly straightforward. But the policy allowing refugees access to the country has opened up a can of worms. Emotions run high in Denmark as soon as the issue of political refugees is brought up in the media and it often is. Some people passionately believe that Denmark should be a safe haven for persecuted people from all over the world, others claim that all refugees are phonies sponging on the Danish welfare system and should be kicked out. You can imagine the kind of discussions that materialise when two such opponents meet in a television studio – it is not a pretty sight.

How Many Foreigners Are There?

As of 2002, there were 259,301 foreign citizens with resident status in Denmark. That is about 4.9% of the population. If you add recently naturalized Danish citizens and children of foreigners, the number is 415,331 or 7.9% of the people in Denmark, who are of immediate foreign descent. By all standards this is a small percentage. For all the discussions in the country about foreigners and refugees Denmark is still for all practical purposes an extremely homogeneous society.

YOUR FIRST IMPRESSIONS

Once you arrive in Denmark your impressions will be totally subjective. Many foreigners love their visit and the American ambassador at one time went on record to proclaim Denmark his favourite country. The rich history, the democratic and humanitarian tradition, and the Danish input into international efforts to install peace and equality in South Africa, the former Yugoslavia and the Middle East formed the basis for his opinion.

Denmark has indeed spruced up its international image lately. Although there are relatively few resources spent on infrastructural investment the two main arrival points – Kastrup Airport and the main terminal for rail traffic in downtown Copenhagen have recently been completely refurbished.

31

Around Copenhagen the general appearance is one of age. There are few modern building complexes, the old ones are kept in livable condition but they are rarely fully renovated or replaced due to the general economic stagnation and a policy of rental controls that makes it difficult for owners to raise money for maintenance.

I often visit the Ornithological Society in Denmark, their Copenhagen office is in a building on Vesterbrogade not too far from the main train station. In that office are two old black and white photographs – one showing the building and the street in 1933, the other in 1913 – and it looks just as it does today in both pictures.

In the suburbs conditions are similar, there are few new buildings but here most homes are occupant owned and well maintained. In fact, in towns and in the countryside the overall impression the foreigner will have of Denmark is one of neatness. You notice it even in the air from the plane while you approach for landing, every square metre

Only the mode of transportation has changed over the years on this Copenhagen street. The towns and cities of Denmark have retained much of their old world charm through the preservation of buildings such as these.

seems to be accounted for and fenced off and utilised. Even on closer inspection you will see how everything is taken care of. Hedges are meticulously cut, gardens are tidy, the roads and buildings are old and worn but well-kept. There are no pot-holes or funny pipes or wires sticking out anywhere. You have obviously come to a highly organised place.

The atmosphere of age, tradition and continuity prevails in Denmark. Arriving from a more dynamic place abroad is equivalent to venturing into a rainforest in the tropics – you instantly have a sense that you are entering into a static and eternal realm, some ancient environment where time has come to a standstill, like in an Einstein experiment. Life goes on here as it seemingly has forever, regardless of developments outside. Of course the perception is not totally correct, it just appears that way.

When I moved back to Denmark I walked into the bank where I had opened up my first account with my savings as a little boy 30 years ago. I had kept an account there all through the years by correspondence. The branch was in the same building on the same street, the furniture had been rearranged, the counters were different, they had computers now. But when a man came up to serve me it struck me that I had seen him before. It dawned on me that this was the same person who had served me 30 years ago! It was almost spooky, I had the feeling that he recognised me. A year later the man had retired, and the bank closed this branch in a restructuring move shortly afterwards.

SOME SUBJECTIVE GENERALISATIONS

Describing a whole people at large in general terms is naturally a dangerous business, it is easy to fall into a trap of stereotyping. However, the environment in which people grow up influences them. Climate and conditions are not the same on Iceland as they are on Barbados, so when people grow up on a cold and treeless island fishing and raising sheep they develop different traits than those who grow up in the tropics cutting sugar cane. Climate, social context, history and culture mark each single individual and these differences are the cause of culture shock when you move abroad and face another set of values.

But even within each nation there are so many different personalities that identifying the common traits must be done carefully and with plenty of reservations. So with the risk of stereotyping let me share with you some of my personal impressions of what the Danes are like.

The Danes are quite interested in foreign affairs and they quickly develop a set of opinions which they strongly defend in heated arguments. Sometimes it appears a bit arbitrary how this opinion was formed but once it is in place it is defended vigorously and small details like new facts are of lesser interest. A Danish politician went on record replying to an opponent, "If those are the facts I deny facts."

I remember shortly after my arrival being lectured by a Danish acquaintance on the conditions in Japan and the nature of the Eastern mentality. I am no expert on Japan, but I have through the years consulted for many Japanese firms, I have been there several times for meetings and cooperated closely with Japanese personnel. I felt a little bit funny being lectured on Eastern mentality by somebody who had once attended an international conference in Tokyo. So, don't be surprised if the Dane you meet knows more about your country than you do!

In my experience many Danes are easy to talk to, friendly and helpful but they do not usually converse much with strangers. Two people who pass each other on some remote road might not even look at each other let alone say hello. If you greet a stranger with a "good morning" don't be surprised if he meets you with some blank stare like you do not exist. If you ride the public bus, notice how most people sit quietly and stare out into empty space, they don't talk much and looking at each other is considered rude.

Strangely enough the same people can be the exact opposite in a crowd where they know each other. They never stop talking for a second and as an outsider you might start to wonder after a few hours how they can keep on thinking of new things to say.

An Indian Anthropologist

The Indian anthropologist, G. Pakash Reddy, studied a village in Jutland a few years back. He went into the community, like a Westerner would enter an Indian village, and in a reverse study examined the local settlement in every detail. The results are published in the book *Danes Are Like That* and make quite intriguing reading.

One of Reddy's first observations was the reserved nature of the villagers. He positioned himself on a bench in the village centre, expecting people to automatically come across to talk to him like they would do in any Asian village. Nobody came. To meet the Danes he systematically had to go around knocking on each door in the hamlet – not to drop in for a chat but to make a formal appointment to come back at some given time for a formal interview. Even then he had to penetrate a thick layer of suspicion and insecurity before he managed to extract the information he needed for his study. By that time he also met some fine people who ended up eventually treating him as a member of the family – but it took a long time.

A Reserved People

If you do start some small-talk conversation with a stranger you might be in luck, some Danes will catch on, they may be flattered or impressed that you would do something they usually don't and you might find a new friend. But don't be too disappointed if the stranger doesn't reply or tells you to mind your own business.

Travelling as a tourist may be one thing but getting along in the Danish working environment is another. For a few years I lived in the United Kingdom working out on the North Sea, travelling to different

35

oil rigs to do contract work. On one contract in the Danish sector I visited Esbjerg in Jutland on route to the rig with two American friends. They were native Texans who wouldn't usually venture out of state, let alone abroad and they were not impressed. They immediately tried to strike up conversations with people we met at the hotel and in the bar later that night and they were not happy with the response. I had to intervene and explain to them that it was nothing personal and that Danes were usually reticent and unresponsive.

On the rig only a few days later we were busily connecting up our equipment on the wellhead when I overhead one of the local rig hands say to his friends, "Don't help these guys unless they give you some cigars or stickers." (Promotional stickers that many oil-rig workers collect.)

Danes returning from abroad often make the same old remark: "People there were so friendly." I have heard it from people returning from all over the world. Turning that around – if you grow up in such a place and come to regard courteous behaviour as the norm rather than the exception and you then move to Denmark how would you find the people? Alternatively I have also heard settlers praise the friendly nature of the Danes – they were Russian refugees which may tell you something about conditions in Russia!

Everybody is Equal

In business and in social life connections don't matter as much as they might in some other countries. There is little corruption, so you cannot really buy favours or speed up applications or transactions, everybody waits their turn. There is all through society a consensus that everybody is equal or should aim to be equal.

As a side effect the noble equality dream has a tendency to create intolerance towards those who do not want to be equal - especially those who want to be better or, worse still, richer. A shipowner who is one of the few rich people in Denmark told a magazine recently that he had to sell off his Rolls Royce and buy a more ordinary looking car

as he got tired of getting 'the finger' by fellow drivers every time he moved through the traffic.

The Danes have a term called *Janteloven* or the 'Law of Jante,' created in a 1933 novel by a Danish/Norwegian writer. It is often quoted in public debate and basically consists of ten commands, boiling down to, "You are no better than we are." However, this trait is not unique to Denmark. In Britain there is a similar sentiment, a certain scepticism or even hostility amongst some groups towards successful individuals. In Australia it is called 'the tall poppy' syndrome, and the cutting down of tall poppies is supposedly a national pastime.

Another side-effect of this 'equality-complex' is the reluctance to serve. If there are to be no masters there should be no servants either. An Asian friend of mine who always flies first class around the world once hesitantly asked me what I thought of SAS, the Scandinavian Airline System. When I commented that the service was the usual sullen Nordic style she seemed somewhat elated, "Oh, I thought it was because I was Asian they behaved like that." I assured her that the cabin crews were not racists, everybody gets the same service in Scandinavia. Regardless of race and religion, we all get bossed around by the employees.

Homogeneous and Uniform

Traditionally Danish society is relatively uniform and it develops slowly. When I was five or six-years-old I saw a black man on the street of Copenhagen; I couldn't believe it, I had heard they existed but I had never seen somebody with coloured skin before! Just as there are places where no white man has ever ventured, the reverse is the case, or it was 35 years ago, in Denmark. Even today there are many communities little affected by foreign influence, especially in some boroughs far from the capital.

Since most Danes grow up in a homogeneous environment speaking the same language and meeting the same kind of people, they develop a familiarity with each other that is quite unusual. Linguistically the Danes, until a few years back, would address strangers in a more polite term – "De" instead of "Du" – for "you." It was like saying Mister or Madam, a dignified approach that created a cordial distance between people. Today this term is out of fashion, although it is still used by some older people or when addressing certain business clients or royalty.

It is a bit of a paradox that the Danes do not relate much to strangers but when they do there are few barriers between them. In the train the conductor might greet you as if the two of you have been chums forever with a jovial and silly remark that is quite funny but just watch out if there is something wrong with your ticket.

Familiarity Can Breed Contempt

Being buddies with everybody is great of course but in Denmark this is often used as a license for everybody to treat everybody else as they please. Since there is a high degree of uniformity, unusual behaviour is instantly spotted and it is normally not appreciated, Danes like things the way they are and they don't take kindly to what they see as changes, interference or mistakes.

I had not ridden a bicycle for many years before moving to Denmark and it was something I looked forward to doing there. In

Denmark there is a great network of bicycle tracks along the roads, the terrain is level and varied and the weather is cool. So I bought a ten-speed bicycle and enjoyed my morning ride to the office except that I had to be aware of my fellow riders to a degree that I had not expected.

One morning I was travelling along on a lovely track, the beach and the cold blue sea was on one side, the green beech forests on the other, the sun was shining from a bright, pale blue sky. In front of me was a young girl riding, her long, blond hair waiving in the breeze. You couldn't find a more picturesque Nordic setting anywhere. I passed her when the road was clear and heard a harsh voice behind me shouting out, "What's the matter, buster, your bell doesn't work?" I was so surprised, I didn't know if I was supposed to answer, so I just sped off. I found out later that it is excepted that you ring your bell before you pass somebody on the track.

I have lost count of how many times I have been scolded like that while bicycling: for not making room while I was being passed; for not giving a signal when I turned; for not using the appropriate lights at night and so on. For some reason a traffic situation always brings the worst out in people and in Denmark that includes bicycling.

But I have also been scolded by the bus driver for not knowing that you have to press a certain button if you want to disembark with a baby-carrier and by fellow travellers for having too much luggage with me. At the post office I was once chewed out for not knowing which form to use and at the badminton court I was reprimanded for warming up the wrong way.

I once rented a canoe near Himmelbjerget in Jutland and went sailing with my two older boys. This is about the closest you can come to a wilderness in Denmark and we were far from the pier on a remote lake when I thought it would be fun to cut through a bunch of straws growing into the water near the bank. "YOU MUST NOT ENTER THE REEDS," a voice roared from afar instantly. It was like some big brother's voice out of nowhere. A fellow tourist nearby had watched us and protested against this serious infringement of protective nature legislation, apparently the reed-beds were off limits to boats.

The Danes all seem to know what to do all the time and they have little patience with those who don't. And since they all feel equal and familiar they don't mind telling each other off.

I mention this for the benefit of other newcomers who may think that they are the only ones getting this treatment. The Danes don't speak to you like that because you are dark-skinned or Asian or female or have red hair or sit in a wheelchair or don't know the language. The Danes don't discriminate – they do that to everybody!

Some Universal Values

Many years back when I started working in China I was briefed on arrival by my colleague, an American. This was in 1982 and China was just opening up for foreign business. My friend had been on location for a few days and wanted to enlighten me on the finer points of dealing with the Chinese. "And when you sit with them make sure your head is always lower than theirs," he advised, "this is a sign of respect." I couldn't believe it when we went for a meeting and he actually crouched down into an unnatural position when he addressed our local partners. My eager-to-please colleague was run out of China a year later but that is a different story.

That kind of social adaptation is absurd and will not even be appreciated by your counterpart, who these days is quite likely to know your background well. In my experience what is always appreciated is a bit of commonsense and consideration. Goodwill and dignity mixed with some self-assured humility is held in high esteem everywhere, including Denmark.

If you adopt a polite and even somewhat aloof style you will be better treated yourself and you will be more effective in dealing with the Danes. Courteous and respectful behaviour is highly regarded.

HOW THE DANES WILL VIEW YOU

As we saw in the first chapter, ties have historically been close with the other Scandinavian and Nordic countries. They have so much in common – so what are the differences? If you come to Denmark from another Nordic country how are you likely to be received? Well, stereotyping is abundant here but to sum up, there is generally a lot of sympathy in Denmark towards Norwegians. They are seen as a somewhat rural people, struggling hard against a tough natural environment and not a threat of any kind. Norway is not really that rural these days and, with the new oil-based wealth, quite advanced, but that is of little relevance to the Danes. Iceland falls into the same category, Finland to some extent also, although it is regarded as slightly more remote, even culturally with its different language and Slavic ties. People from here will, however, always be well received in Denmark.

The Danes are adapting to the new multicultural society but for a race of traditionally blonde, blue eyed people, dark skin can still be a curious sight. (Photo: Jens Henriksen)

Sweden

Sweden is a special case. Although there is a lot of traditional admiration in Denmark for Swedish technology and know-how, this close neighbour is also viewed with a portion of ridicule and some envy.

Ridicule because of the disciplined and formal nature of society and especially because of the rigorous liquor laws that many Swedes travel to Zealand to escape. (In Sweden the sale of beer and liquor is rigorously controlled, so when Swedes land in Denmark they tend to overdo it, sometimes making complete fools of themselves after a heavy night on the town.)

Envy because Sweden is a larger, bigger and more prosperous country with a successful car and aircraft industry and with many internationally known sportsmen and entertainers. With the crisis in recent years in the Swedish financial markets and welfare programmes, this envy might diminish.

Germany

To the south of Denmark lies the big neighbour, Germany. Shortly after World War II there was a lot of hostility amongst Danes towards the German people. Germany had been devestatingly bombed, was desperately poor and somewhat looked down upon in subsequent years.

Money, however, always commands respect and that came with the subsequent German rebuilding and prosperity. German society modified with economic success, it is today less totalitarian and disciplined and, especially after reunification, there is more sympathy in Denmark towards the Germans. Many Danes speak the language quite fluently, especially in southern Jutland, where they receive German television, and on the west coast which is frequented by hundreds of thousands of Germans coming there for holidays every year.

Britain

The British are generally well liked in Denmark. There is still some admiration towards this formerly grand European nation, it is the only English-speaking country in Europe, so many Danes go there to improve their language skills. London, especially, is a popular place to stay for short or long periods of time. British visitors to Denmark behave in the correct manner and are generally well received, although fanatic football supporters might be an exception.

United States

The United States is of course a special case. During the Cold War Americans were disliked by many Danes for their perceived aggressive and warmongering conduct internationally and their lack of civil rights at home. There were frequently demonstrations against the States and the official Danish alliance with that nation through NATO (North Atlantic Treaty Organisation). American tourists were often somewhat ridiculed for their loud clothes, lack of cultural knowledge and super-friendly gestures.

All this has, to some extent, mellowed. There is the usual absorption of American culture; American actors, actresses, musicians and sportsmen are worshipped, just like everywhere else in the world. American fast-food stores occupy prime Copenhagen real estate, as they do in all big cities. American visitors are looked up to, like they are most places, although in Denmark there is also a strong awareness that all is not well in the United States – local poverty and Third World conditions in some states are often covered by the Danish media.

Continental Europe

Southern Europe is perceived with mixed feelings in Denmark. Spain, France and Greece are where you go for vacation and southern Germany is something you trade with or pass through on the autobahn. Those areas as well as Italy and Portugal are still regarded as the backward Catholic countries they were 40 years ago. Well, they are still mainly Catholic but they are no longer backward. They are fully developed economically and socially, complete with high divorce rates and social welfare and budget deficits that once used to be exclusive to northern Europe. That hasn't really sunk into the Danish mind yet, so Danes become perpetually surprised when they go down and find out how far southern Europe has come.

Eastern Europe tends to be viewed as one block, although the stages in social and economic development obviously are enormously different from country to country. With more contacts and tourism and trade this perception will of course change.

If you visit Denmark from a Third World country you may find that there are two camps amongst the Danes you meet. One group of Danes cherish everything foreign, they find drums from Africa and chopsticks from Asia so charming and they boil over with sympathy for you. The other group of people are sceptical, to them these foreigners belong at home, and the foreign ministry is wasting too much money trying in vain to help them. There is very little direct racism and hatred towards foreigners in Denmark, but be prepared for some cynicism.

A CULTURE UNDERGOING CHANGE

Contrary to how it might initially appear, Denmark is not a static society, things are happening, and the nation is opening up to the outside world.

All countries had to re-evaluate their status with the end of the Cold War in 1989 and Denmark was no exception. The world is converging into some kind of consensus that socialism doesn't work and now there are signs that the welfare state doesn't either. Free markets don't solve all the problems and as more information is shared amongst countries these days, international cooperation is clearly the way to go.

In 1995 Sweden together with Finland decided to join the EU. In the meantime the debate about how far and how fast the EU should integrate goes on and on. One way or another the Union will change shape, and more nations to the east are standing by to join it and NATO as well. A massive expansion of the EU will happen in 2004 when 10 former eastern block members join the union, later also Bulgaria and Rumania, possibly Turkey. That leaves only Switzerland, Norway and the former Yugoslavia outside. Denmark is developing closer trade links with East Asia to tap into the explosive economic growth going on there. These new ties will gradually change the culture of Denmark, so stay tuned.

A ROYAL COMPLAINT

In February 2002 Prince Henrik (seen walking behind his wife on page 52) complained to the daily mass-circulation tabloid *B.T.* that after having lived in Denmark for 35 years – 30 of these as prince – he still felt neglected and humiliated by the Danes. He made this remark after he had been by-passed to perform an official duty, which was eventually assigned to Crown Prince Frederik. So, if the Queen's husband, after one generation, still does not feel accepted and integrated to Danish society... what hope does that offer to other newcomers?

Chapter Three

MEDIA AND POLITICS

What a people think of themselves and their world is reflected in the media. But not only is it reflected there, these days it is largely determined by the media. In Denmark the media, as in so many other Western countries, has taken on a life of its own. The mass media has grown out of its traditional role as only a mirror of society, reporting on events. In Denmark the media is much more powerful than that. Journalists set the agenda of public attention and debate and greatly influence developments.

THE PRESS

There are no less than 32 daily papers in Denmark today, although that figure has actually come down a lot in recent years, from a high of 85 in 1960, but it is still an incredible number for such a small nation. However, most papers are local and have small circulations, only five daily papers in the whole country have a print run of over 100,000. Seventy-five percent of the adult population in Denmark reads a paper every day.

Among the big five there is tough competition. Three of the main papers are fairly serious morning editions while the other two are small format tabloids appearing later in the morning. They are each produced by a major publishing house and they are fighting a pitched battle for readers.

The Danish tabloids are not much different from their counterparts elsewhere – they are mostly big headlines with a sensational slant and little substance. But often they focus on certain issues and by whipping up public outrage and by pestering the responsible politicians they make events happen, which they in turn can report on in some self sustaining cycle.

Basically the tabloids give the impression that they will run any story that makes a buck. And since they appeal to the lower instincts in people the famous headline from *The Sun* in Britain – "Up yours, Delors" (Mr Jacques Delors was then head of the EU Commission) is easily matched in vulgarity by Danish editors. This kind of approach to important issues unfortunately permeates all through the Danish media and can be quite shocking. In the written media journalists clearly take a stand in their reporting – they don't just report, they campaign for one cause or another.

LISTENING TO THE RADIO

On Danish radio, journalists are not content with just seeking out the facts and sharing them with the listener – they call up the top person concerned and debate with him or her. This is again indicative of the

Danish view of equality and anyone coming to Denmark from a more totalitarian environment will marvel at how easily journalists get access to information. On the other hand, this kind of journalism blurs the line between reporting facts and commenting on them and these interviews often turn into unpleasant arguments but of course the Danes don't mind this – they love a good argument.

TELEVISION

After having been under tight state control since introduction, the electronic media was liberalised in Denmark in 1986. Today the state-run DR and the partly private TV2 run neck-to-neck in the competition for viewers, the purely commercial stations TV3 and TV Denmark plus some smaller regional stations fight over the smaller percentages. There are now nine different news programmes each evening reporting much the same things in the same way.

In Denmark 99.5% of households have a television, 28% have two or more, and 54% have a video cassette recorder. The average Dane watches around three hours of television every day. A quarter of viewers can see a foreign station beamed directly from a neighbouring country; in the east from Sweden, in the south from Germany and in the north from Norway. Apart from that, another almost 70.6% of viewers have access to satellite television via cable or dish, so channels like Discovery, MTV, CNN and Childrens Channel have long been household terms in Danish homes.

However, in spite of the excellent international choice most Danes prefer to see their own, locally produced television. Romantic comedies from the fifties and sixties, Christmas shows, national soccer games, "Danish Melody Grand Prix," "News at Nine," game shows and celebrity talk-shows inevitably make up the top ten list of the most watched shows every year. These are all locally produced shows in the Danish language. Only rarely does a famous Hollywood produced movie sneak in at the bottom of the list. The Danes cherish the old stuff and many programmes are repeated again and again.

Watching Television

It is always fun to watch a new country's television. The commercials alone give you some idea of what the local values and humour are like.

Many programmes of course are imported. Within the EU this is an issue which is often debated. But since they are cheap, entertaining and professionally produced, it is unlikely that there will be an embargo on foreign television.

Danish news programmes can be pretty dry and focus very much on local news and, rather than run through the latest developments, they tend to get lost in lengthy background analysis, so that after a while you are not sure if you are watching a news broadcast or an all night discussion by a panel of experts. For the best coverage of world events switch to CNN or the BBC.

Danish journalists are, however, good at investigative reporting and if you pick up the language you will enjoy some of the magazine style programmes that they produce. No stone is left unturned when they go after scandal or corruption.

Coverage of Events Abroad

If, however, you watch a programme about your own country and don't quite recognise it, don't be surprised. In Denmark every person is born with a firm opinion on all topics, or so it seems. They then select and arrange the facts so that they fit and confirm these beliefs.

This is largely reinforced through the media coverage in Denmark which focuses on disasters and misfortunes in other countries. If people do not die there is no news and the more who die the bigger the news. So you hear a lot about Rwanda, Afghanistan, Iraq and all the other trouble spots of the world. You also hear about executions, whippings, terrorism, plane crashes and natural disasters abroad. When Singapore announced that they now had a GNP per capita larger than their former colonial power, Great Britain, I thought that it was a fairly interesting turn of events, but it didn't make the Danish news!

Consequently, Danes tend to view the countries outside of the EU as less fortunate and comfortable than themselves. I mention this because it is important for the newcomer to realise that if you want to communicate in Denmark about conditions in your old country you have to break through a wall of preconceptions and stereotypes first. And it is very likely that you are not going to succeed.

In Japan they say that part of what pushes the Japanese forward is the conception – the misconception as it is – that they still have a lot of catching up to do. We know that the Japanese long ago achieved a standard of living and to some extent also a quality of life equal to or superior to the West but many Japanese people are not so sure of that, so they are reluctant to slow down. In our family our youngest son constantly compares himself to his two older brothers, who are always a few steps ahead of him – it drives him forward because he always sees himself as inferior, although he is actually doing very well for his age. In Denmark the opposite is the case. Since the public at large has a distorted view of conditions abroad they think that they are still top of the heap and the media keeps confirming this outdated notion, while the outside world is often racing past them.

It may help that more and more Danes travel abroad now, not just on the usual package tours to Spain and Paris but also further afield. Backpacking is the 'in' way of going, you are then not a tourist – you are a traveller seeking to immerse yourself in the foreign culture. The foreign ministry even finances such travellers on condition that they report back about their trip when they return – the state will also give you part of your salary while you are away as a sabbatical benefit to reduce unemployment. All in all a pretty neat deal.

This may slowly contribute to a more balanced view of the outside world amongst Danes. And then again it may not, some travellers incredible as it may seem, somehow manage to return with their misconceptions reinforced.

Probably more effective than state manipulated aid and travel is the trade and co-production ventures with the Third World that the

Danish private sector is embarking on these days. One of the positive side effects of such relationships is the way communications are improved, barriers are broken down and international interdependence is enhanced. If you speak to Danes you might find that the ones with a convincing understanding of conditions abroad are the people who have participated in this process.

CELEBRITY WORSHIPPING

People everywhere like celebrities and Denmark is no exception. If anything, celebrities are celebrated in Denmark more than anywhere else. Celebrated, gossiped about, ogled, put on a pedestal – and pulled down again! It is a paradox that in a country where equality is promoted throughout society there should be such a fascination in the media with people who are different and above the rest for one reason or another.

Just look at any news vendor and see the variety of glossy magazines featuring celebrities, the five most sold magazines all belong to this category and are printed each week in an incredible total of 1,280,000 copies. On top of that comes a number of ladies' weeklies and monthlies and magazines about motoring and boating and hunting and home-making and gardening and food and money and exercise and any other topic you can think of. More than 40 weekly or monthly magazines are printed in Denmark, an incredible selection for such a small country.

The Royal Family

The royal family is always featured prominently in magazines. Denmark is a parliamentary democracy, but it has maintained the monarchistic element of its constitution. This family is a remnant from feudal times and is outside of democratic control. Its wealth and power is inherited from generation to generation and the Danish people are fascinated with it. The royal family is generally quite respected too and there have been none of the traumatic crises of mistrust and family break-ups that have plagued the British Royal Family and brought the monarchy as an institution within the Commonwealth up for debate.

At the moment Denmark is ruled by a Queen, Margrethe II. She is married to Prince Henrik of Denmark who is of French descent, the media inevitably pokes fun of his heavy foreign accent. They have two handsome and bright sons, Frederik and Joachim – the darlings of the gossip magazines, their every move is covered in living colour. This is particularly true of Frederik, since he is the oldest and the crown prince. Of exceptional interest is of course any romantic links Frederik may form.

Queen Margrethe II is often seen performing official duties and along with the other members of the royal family maintains a high profile. (Photo: Jens Henriksen)

In 1995 however, it was Joachim who stole the limelight for a while when he married a beautiful young woman from Hong Kong, and the media had a field day. Although there is a tradition of royals marrying foreigners, this selection is usually restricted to those within Northern Europe. This was the first time that a Danish royal had married an Asian. Apart from the fact that the new princess must have possessed some qualities that the young prince could not find amongst girls at home, the very circumstance that Joachim met her while being stationed for A.P. Møller in Hong Kong is indicative of East Asia's rising economic and cultural clout.

Her Royal Highness Margrethe's mother passed away in 2000, but the Queen has a few sisters and other family members who all qualify to have their every move shadowed by the society journalists. There is an elaborate system of rank within this high society hierarchy with the royal family at the top, appointed ministers just below (ministers in Denmark do not have to be elected members of parliament), then high court judges.

The rest of the nobility, generals and top civil servants down to the premier lieutenants at the bottom of the ladder make up the numbers and since there are few new-rich entrepreneurs in Denmark, this group of people, who have either inherited their status or made it by pushing paper for decades, constitutes the Danish upper class. They are the aristocracy and the establishment. They gather on occasions for dinners and parties and give each other promotions and commendation every year. And you can be sure that the society writers and photographers will be there to tell the common folks all about it.

The Rich and Famous

To be a somebody in any society you either have to be influential, knowledgeable or skilful, entertaining or just plain old boring rich – and Denmark is no exception. Since there are few rich people and knowledge is generally well distributed, most somebodies are entertainers and politicians (who tend to double up as entertainers).

Wealth is very evenly distributed in Denmark. Denmark does not hold many world records - but it is said to be the hardest country in the world to save money in. Some families, however, have succeeded in spite of this, although only 22 have assets in the one hundred million dollars and above category. The largest family-owned fortune belongs to Mærsk Mc-Kinney Møller and his family, of Mærsk and A.P. Møller fame. Their container ships with the white and blue star logo can be seen in ports all over the world and the family fortune is US$3.3 billion. But they were temporarily overtaken in 1995 by another household name at least among families with kids – Lego. This very successful toy manufacturer is owned by the family of Christiansen, for a few years the richest in Denmark. In spite of their wealth this family keeps a fairly low profile in Danish public life.

After these two there is a large jump down the ladder to the Clausen family, who owns Danfoss, which makes refrigerator compressors and thermostat valves, with assets of US$1.0 billion. Then comes a long list of family owned businesses in manufacturing, construction, building materials, banking, publishing and retailing, down to one of the newcomers, Lars Larsen, who recently made a fortune selling quilts and other household items and running a package tour travel agency, and who just squeezes into the official one hundred million dollar group in spite of occasional rumours in the media that he is actually insolvent.

Most of these businesses are old money and the Wedell family's holdings, currently at US$120 million go back 12 generations to 1672. Most of the other business empires were founded before the Second World War, many back in the 19th century. That in spite of some tough inheritance laws in Denmark, which required heirs to hand up to 80-90% of the family fortune over to the state as they were passed on to the next generation. This has wiped out much of the farming-based aristocracy, so that the people who are rich and famous today are the ones who diversified, moved abroad or hid the money in family funds exempt from taxes. Under pressure to stop the loss of capital the government in 1995 modified the inheritance legislation so that direct descendants (sons and daughters) now pay only 15% in tax. More distant relatives pay 36% when they inherit the family business.

Rags-to-riches characters who find themselves in the tabloids every time they appear in public include Mrs Janni Spies, the secretary who married an eccentric businessman and then squandered his 140 million dollar travel agent empire away on bad investments after his death. Since she managed to marry into another wealthy family (Christian Kjær, of FLS Industries) before she went broke, she is still assured of a permanent place in the public eye.

Another story involves a businessman cum politician (Klaus Riskjær Petersen) who made a name for himself as a guru of the young 'greed-is-good' crowd of ambitious entrepreneurs and MBA students who flourished in the 1980s. Riding high on his popularity, built on risky investments, leveraged buy-outs and a generally extravagant lifestyle Riskjær Petersen got himself elected to the European Parliament through an American style, big spending election campaign. Then his investments turned sour, his holding company collapsed under a heap of bad debt and the police started investigations into his affairs. Suddenly Mr Petersen was not as popular any more and his career as a politician came to an end, although lately, he appears to be clawing back to fame and fortune. How? In the Internet business, of course!

Sport and Politics

The Danes love their sports personalities and many Danish athletes are the best in the world within their sports, especially in soccer, badminton, cycling and sailing. A good performance in the sporting world assures you a place in the Danish media – for a while anyway. While the cultural stars may stay in the news for decades, the sportsperson often fades away as soon as another one comes in and wins the next championship.

Apart from the rich, the most influential people are the politicians. The Danes love talking politics and the country is awash with 'political animals' thriving in this environment. Since the media makes or breaks you in politics, well-known television personalities are virtually assured a seat in parliament should they decide to run. Just as a former actor in the United States made it to the nation's highest office in 1980, so Uffe Elleman-Jensen in Denmark rose to fame and influence with a television background.

Mr Elleman was a popular economics commentator before being elected a member of parliament and appointed foreign minister. He was later mentioned as a candidate for the prime minister's post. He lost narrowly in the 1998 election, by just a few votes, and retired from politics in disgust.

Another, slightly more grotesque example occurred at the election in 1994, when for the first time a person with no political affiliations was elected to parliament. This man, Jakob Haugaard, was the local village joker who stood for election as a prank. His programme called for better weather on Sundays and bigger Christmas presents for everybody. The media loved him and he ended up pulling 23,253 votes, sufficient to get elected, and suddenly he was in the national and even international limelight. Mainly a creation of the media, he did not accomplish much as a Member of Parliament, and in 1998, he retired to pursue a more successful career as an entertainer.

In Denmark the quality of politicians is often considered to be low and few elected representatives emerge with statesmanship qualities and visionary authority. This is partly because the salaries of politicians and appointed ministers are low compared to other countries. A busy sales executive in Denmark can make more money than the minister of defence. Politicians are also roughly treated by the public, often scorned and ridiculed and sometimes pelted with eggs and tomatoes. So talented visionaries in Denmark prefer to go into business, the sciences or the arts where they are treated with more respect.

World Famous Danes

Making it on the local scene in Denmark is of course not equivalent to international fame but a few Danes have become well known abroad. You will find that many foreigners have heard about them, although they may not know exactly who they are.

The following names are some of the more significant contributors to Danish notoriety.

Hans Christian Andersen (1805–1875). Probably the most famous of all Danes and rightly so. Writer of fairytales for children, often the stories had a deeper, slightly tragic significance meant for grownups. Try to read some.

Bille August. Movie Director who won the 1989 Academy Award in the best non-American film category for his movie *Pelle the Conqueror* based on a novel by the Danish writer Martin Andersen Nexø. The movie is great – catch it if you can.

Badminton Players. Especially throughout Asia, Denmark is renowned in badminton. I have lost count of the number of times I have been able to break the ice with Asians I have met when they said, "Oh, your name is Morten, like Morten Frost" (who was riding high on the badminton Grand Prix circuit for a number of years). Other All-England winners like Lene Køppen, Ib Frederiksen and Poul Høyer Larsen are also remembered – though not for long.

Karen Blixen (1885–1962). A writer who had her modern breakthrough when Meryl Streep personified her in an award winning Hollywood production of her autobiography, *Out of Africa.*

Niels Bohr (1885–1962). This scientist was a contemporary of Karen Blixen's. A great nuclear physicist and Nobel Prize winner in 1922 for his work on atomic particles, Bohr went to the States in 1942 and worked on the American Atomic Bomb project. As a dedicated humanitarian and visionary he met Roosevelt and Churchill and pleaded with them to share research with the Russians to avoid antagonism after the Second World War. That was before the first atomic device had even been tested. As we all know his advice was neglected and 40 years of destructive arms-race followed. Bohr's son, Aage, also won the Nobel Prize for physics, in 1975.

Victor Borge (1909–2000). Classical pianist and comical entertainer. This unlikely combination won him a large audience abroad and especially in the United States.

Football Players. Stars change all the time of course, so please fill in the current names from the national squad yourself. My own favourite was the 166 centimetre tall Allan Simonsen who played for German and Spanish teams in the seventies and eighties and who became European Footballer of the Year in spite of his small physique. The Laudrup brothers (Michael playing for Real Madrid and Brian for Glasgow Rangers) and Peter Schmeichel (goalkeeper with Manchester United) are the current hot names.

Hamlet, Prince of Denmark. A mythical figure that Shakespeare introduced in his play of the same name which is now the most played performance in the theatre world. The play takes place in Elsinore which is Helsingør in northern Zealand and includes the immortal words, "To be or not to be …."

Søren Kirkegaard (1813–1855). Philosopher and poet. Controversial at his time, Kirkegaard's thinking has had something of a renaissance amongst some students in modern times.

Gitte Nielsen. Rumour has it that Miss Nielsen went to the hotel of Sylvester Stallone and sent a picture of herself up to his room with a note; "Would you like to meet me?". He would, and although the marriage of course didn't last long Mrs Stallone-Nielsen was assured fame in the Hollywood backdrop. One of many such blonde and blue-eyed Danish girls who travel to California to make it in the movies or to marry well.

Jørn Utzon. Architect. His claim to fame was designing the Sydney Opera House in Australia, although he actually didn't quite finish this controversial project. Has also designed the Kuwait Parliament which was destroyed during the Gulf War and many other grand buildings.

THE POLITICAL SYSTEM

Politics in Denmark is more than just a necessary decision making process, it provides countless hours of entertainment and discussion for the public. While pop stars and television personalities are treated like people of importance, the politicians are treated like entertainers. In the media world there is a merging of the two, so it can be difficult to decide exactly which is which.

In spite of the constant bickering over details there are signs that most Danes are actually quite happy with things the way they are. Less than five percent of the voters are members of a political party and fewer still participate actively in formulating policies. The political parties have come to depend on public funds to even exist. At the

59

moment each party receives 85 cents per vote per year, which will soon be increased to $US2.50.

The political structure in itself in quite simple: The parliament has 179 seats. Elections can be called at any time but must be held at least every four years. At the moment eight political parties are represented, two of which form a minority government under a prime minister from the largest of the parties, Venstre.

It is unlikely for one single party to hold the majority power, as is the case in so many other countries. Therefore, Danish politics is a never-ending series of discussions and compromises and the key problems seem to be permanently under review.

The parliament is in session from Tuesday to Friday, outside of school holidays. It is housed within a huge castle, the Christiansborg Palace, constructed in 1736 but rebuilt in 1903. The public is allowed to visit the parliament during sessions and listen to the debate from the balconies in the magnificent chamber, you do not need an appointment or a ticket, there are no queues, no metal detector – just walk in off the street and sit down. (Call (45) 3337 5500 for details of when the parliament is in session. Public tours of the whole building are arranged on most Sundays, call (45) 3392 6492 for details on the tours.)

A wing of the Danish Parliament. The statue is of King Frederick VII

At Christiansborg the parliament represents the legislative force. The ministries, some of which are in other parts of the building complex, execute the laws. The third element in Western democracy, the judiciary, with the High Court is located just around the corner. Although the Queen does not live at Christiansborg (she stays at Amalienborg Palace just down the road a bit) she maintains some official state visitor's rooms in one of the annexes of the palace. Don't miss seeing this centre of Danish power if you are in the neighbourhood, it is really an experience.

Local and Super-National Government

Apart from this national legislative and administrative centre in Copenhagen each district in Denmark has its own rule. It is a system of 14 large counties divided into no less than 275 smaller municipalities. There is also a network of parishes for religious purposes. It is a system dating back to 1662 and which today has become totally antiquated. All Danish decision-makers agree that this cannot go on. But when it comes to how exactly this system should be changed the consensus comes to an end – so reform is impossible and nothing is done about it.

Every four years there are local elections to county and municipality councils. These councils have quite extensive influence over local affairs, liaising closely of course with the national authorities. Hospitals, social services, schools, daycare centres and roads and public housing are under the responsibility of local councils. You do not have to be a Danish citizen to participate in regional elections so many foreigners join in and become active in local politics.

On top of all this comes the super-national structure that has been put in place since Denmark joined the European Community (now Union). Roughly one third of all legislation in the Danish National Parliament today is a direct transcript of laws pushed through the EU system. This union itself is another jungle of bureaucracy involving a directly elected parliament, a powerful commission, a council of

61

ministers and a judiciary wing. It keeps countless numbers of over-paid civil servants busy and makes political and economic reform much harder. However, the EU has also kept the peace in Western Europe for the longest period of time in modern history and for that we should all be thankful.

Referendums

Once in a while there will be a referendum in Denmark. This is an additional tool to be used within the parliamentary democracy. A referendum has to be called if the constitution needs to be amended or if national sovereignty is transferred away from the parliament, as has been the case several times as the Danish membership of the EU has evolved. The parliamentarians can also call for advisory referendums or a 30% minority can demand any legislation to be put before the voters before it is passed. Only the Budget Bill and other financial matters cannot be sent for a referendum.

The old gentlemen who designed the constitution back in 1849 (women did not participate then) very cleverly foresaw that if finances were put to the vote the people would just give themselves fewer taxes and more benefits from the state. As it turned out that was what happened anyway. Voters didn't need referendums, they just voted in governments who promised them an endless stream of free subsidies.

A Shocking Election Campaign

There is a major flaw in Western political administration and nobody knows what to do about it. In this regard it was a major culture shock for me to witness my first televised election campaign in Denmark.

The party representative had just given a strong opening presentation on economic policy. The nation was one hundred billion dollars in the red, in spite of massive taxation rates – the highest in the world. The annual budget deficit would be around seven billion dollars. This had to stop. All very well, anybody of course would agree to that.

Then came questions from the studio audience. An elderly person asked, "Does that mean that my old age pension will be cut?" A young girl said, "I am a student. What does Fremskridtspartiet (the name of the party) think of student grants?" A middle-aged man raised his arm and said more bluntly, "I am unemployed. Do you honestly expect me to vote for you when you are proposing to cut my benefits?"

Since most people in Denmark are either on state benefits, or have children or parents who are, creating a sustainable economy is virtually impossible. I have never heard a single politician during the campaign who dared suggest a balanced budget, he would have been laughed out of the meeting if he had tried. In the meantime debts are piling up.

Political Debate

Although there is a lot of political debate and sometimes nasty arguments going on about which road to take forward, it seems that reduced, public sector debt amounting to 50 % of GDP appears permanent. When it comes to the major issues such as membership of NATO, membership of the EU, the welfare state as a concept or humanitarian issues of human rights and foreign aid to Third World countries, there is a high level of consensus between the members of parliament.

It is especially so now that the Cold War is over and all the ideological jargon of that era has been put to pasture. There is still a left and a right in Danish politics but it is becoming increasingly difficult to see which is which and governments are formed across the spectrum.

What is discussed are all the minor issues, such as the size of the budget cuts, environmental management and refugee policies. Since nobody really wants to rock the boat and take some firm decisions, the problems cannot be solved. So they do not go away and the same debates are performed again and again. It is a frustrating aspect of living in Denmark, but then it is also part of the charm – the old world decadence, the reluctance to change, the protection of the weak that impedes rapid progress, it is all part of the package and you cannot have one without the other.

Chapter Four

THE HUMANITARIAN TRADITION

At our home in Jutland, north of Århus, we are only half an hour's drive from Mols Bjerge, with its rolling hills, grass and heather and scattered coniferous and deciduous woodlands. It is a wonderful place to go hiking with the family. Fully protected, this land is one of many nature reserves and other protected areas located all over Denmark. No less than 4.3% of the country enjoys some sort of protected status.

At Mols there is a visitor's centre with elaborate maps over the area, displays regarding the geology, vegetation and wildlife, exhibitions of stuffed animals and countless leaflets and information forms that can be collected free of charge. There is no attendant at the centre but everything is neat and well maintained.

The Danes cherish their natural environment and in few other countries will you find nature to be so well protected. It is all part of a strikingly different set of values that apart from nature protection includes humanitarianism, egalitarianism, individualism, support for the weak in society and respect for democracy. As a newcomer some of these values will please you, others will shock you.

THE PROTECTION OF NATURE

According to a law that came into effect in 1992, the public can walk or cycle all across the country, even across fields and private beaches and forests, provided they are not fenced off and that nothing on the property is disturbed. On private property you are obliged to follow the trails, if you bring a dog it must be leashed and you can only go during daylight hours and not too near houses.

These are the main rules for moving around natural places in Denmark, in actual fact the legislation and the associated guidelines are very detailed and the Ministry of the Environment has published a booklet with all the minute details. These are designed to keep everybody happy, both landowners and land users.

The Danes have coined an interesting phrase, 'millimetre democracy.' This indicates a way of administrating which aims to ensure that every person gets the same rights and benefits. Nobody must be treated differently, all points of contention or potential contention must be addressed. It is a very time consuming way of ruling that keeps hundreds of thousands of public employees busy designing and interpreting laws and regulations. Naturally, it does not always work and the Danes constantly complain that they are being treated differently and unfairly anyhow. In the case of nature protection, however, it has helped to shackle farmers, hunters and industries, that use nature and have the potential to harm it if not instructed otherwise.

In Denmark the wildlife is carefully protected through legislation that regulates hunting and fishing down to the smallest detail. All hunters must pass a test before they can carry a gun, every single vertebrate species is investigated and many are protected. The hunting season is rigorously enforced and in this respect the Danes are very disciplined and law abiding. At dawn on September 1 every year the rural countryside and the wetlands come alive with a barrage of gunfire as the hunting season on ducks and geese begins.

Exceptions exist for various species of fowl, so that greylag goose can be hunted from August 1 and tufted duck only from October 1. Partridge can be hunted from September 16, the pheasant from October 1 – but only the male, the female is safe until October 16. And although you usually hunt from sun-up to sundown, some birds can be shot on some occasions after sundown, but only during some months. All this might change depending on which county you are in and it is all calculated with millimetre accuracy and, surprisingly enough, the hunters seem to go along with it.

Fishing for sport is similarly regulated, so don't just throw a line into some creek without checking the regulations carefully first. And don't collect tadpoles in the pond nearby your home to have your kids watch them turn into frogs – it is not allowed, all amphibians are protected by law in Denmark. In this last case authorities might not prosecute you if you release the frogs unharmed after a while.

Caring for the Environment

In a wider context the Danes are also stout defenders of the environment. About a quarter of a million people are members of some environmental organisation, the largest being Danmarks Naturfredningsforening (DN) – the Nature Conservation Society of Denmark. Even the hunting lobby, which is almost as strong in terms of members and participants, takes on a green image these days and participates in conservation efforts.

The Danes gang together as soon as a few of them share an interest and form a society, joining one can be a great way for a newcomer to meet new people and integrate into the nation. Joining DN is a good place to start, the society organises day trips to the countryside and

67

tagging along is a convenient and informal way of getting to know Denmark and its inhabitants.

In all social surveys that are published, Danes value a healthy environment highly – even more highly than economic growth. So although the details are being contested there is national consensus to support tough environmental laws.

There are special taxes on energy consumption and carbon dioxide emissions and farmers are under constant pressure to reduce their consumption of fertilisers and insecticides, since these run off the fields and contaminate watercourses, lakes, coastal seas and not least the ground water. Since 99% of the Danish water supply comes from wells drilled into the ground, tapping ground water reservoirs, there is great public concern about keeping the ground free from contamination by chemicals, oil leaks and heavy metals. Apart from reform of the welfare system, environmental problems and how to tackle them seem to be the most extensively covered topic on Danish news programs.

Internationally, Denmark again and again comes forward as a green nation. The private sector has built up an important capacity for environmental technology and know-how which is becoming a valuable export commodity. Denmark is a leading exporter of wind powered generators, energy conservation concepts and equipment and chemical cleanup plants.

Politically, Danish government and non-governmental representatives lobby for tougher air pollution standards and more environmental aid and advice to poorer nations. At the UN environmental conference in Rio in 1992 the richer nations pledged to spend half a percent of their gross national product (GNP) on international environmental aid. Only Denmark is coming close to this goal and will soon provide about 1 billion dollars of its borrowed national deficit on international aid targeted at environmental projects and administered by the Ministry of the Environment (not the Ministry of Foreign Affairs like other aid).

Environmentally friendly wind generators such as these are now being exported by Denmark. (Photo: Lone Eg Nissen)

The commitment to protect nature and the environment is one thing I personally like about the humanitarian tradition in Denmark. Other aspects of this tradition are a little harder to adjust to and some you may find make no sense at all.

LAW AND ORDER

When you first arrive in Denmark you may be surprised, even shocked, at the very liberal attitude towards law and order which prevails. The question of the rights of the criminal overshadowing those of the victim is one which causes a great deal of controversy and

69

which is not easily resolved. Individual examples of crimes and criminals, which test the Danish humanitarian ideal, are commonly debated in the media and in casual conversation but as crime escalates the consensus of opinion seems to be moving towards a tightening of the restrictions placed on criminals. Sometimes though, it seems that Danish liberalism has progressed beyond what is sensible and reached a point from which it is hard to return.

One Sunday morning my children were watching television, there is always a programme on TV2 at this time of the week for kids, with some friendly host doing games and interviews in front of a live audience and showing cartoons in between. His guest that morning was a convict from a Danish prison. I only watched a few minutes of the episode but it showed film clips of how the congenial prisoners went about their daily routines, eating and exercising. Life in prison was presented as pretty appealing and afterwards there were questions from the kids in the audience to our friendly, local criminal who got a chance to advertise his way of life. Finally, I turned the TV off and sent my boys outside to play!

A Constant Fear of Crime

With this casual and permissive attitude, crime rates of course soar and the Danes live with a growing fear of violence and theft. A friend of ours who returned from Kenya was surprised to hear that reported crimes per capita were actually 73 times higher in Denmark than in Kenya. Numbers of reported crimes have more than tripled over the last 30 years to over half a million per year, especially violent crimes, break-ins and thefts. One fifth of all Danish families are affected by crime every year.

Most of it is petty stuff, but it is nevertheless a nuisance. My father-in-law has had eight bicycles stolen in five years, he tries to get old models, just good enough to take him down the road and to work but not so fancy that they would tempt a thief but they disappear all the same.

I quickly noticed how crime was a constant topic at Danish social gatherings. During one of the first dinners we were invited to we met a man who mentioned he had just had his car stolen. Everybody then suddenly chipped in, "My bicycle just disappeared the other day," a lady said. "When I returned home to my apartment in Copenhagen last month it had been totally cleaned out," the man next to her contributed, "thank God I had just arranged insurance."

And therein seems to lie the Danish answer to crime – insurance. Since the perpetrators cannot be effectively dealt with, you simply insure yourself and your belongings. A certain paranoia, however, still prevails. The Danes lock their doors, install burglar alarms and clamp devices across the steering wheels of their cars so they cannot be stolen so easily. In the supermarket you have to deposit a ten-krone coin to get a trolley, otherwise the company is convinced you will run off with it.

HELPING THE WEAK

Nevertheless, you just have to be impressed with the Danish humanitarian tradition. Part of the prevailing philosophy is built upon the belief that humans are basically good – if treated well they will respond and do good to others. It is a noble and admirable concept which is hopefully true in most cases.

Thousands of people in the country firmly believe in at least some aspects of humanitarianism and become engaged in anti-war movements or campaign for better conditions for women, refugees, children, the handicapped, the mentally ill, AIDS victims or drug addicts – every kind of weak (or perceived to be weak) link in society seems to have a support group.

Some groups are volunteers helping out or campaigning in their own time, contributing with privately collected funds. But many others are public employees who join the social services out of idealism. They lobby within the administration and use tax money for their programmes. Ironically, the result in Denmark tends to be that by supporting the weak you often create more weakness. Some studies have made a connection between the availability of welfare or aid to a particular group and an increase in numbers within those groups.

WORKERS' RIGHTS

The labour unions in Europe played an important role during the last century and in the beginning of this one, fighting for workers' rights. They helped transform the typical European factory from an inhumane and dangerous sweatshop to a modern working environment and they greatly improved prosperity for all workers.

In Denmark today many union leaders still have their roots set firmly back in those old days, they sing the same songs and think the same thoughts as people did when Karl Marx and Lenin were alive and well. Most likely when you settle in Denmark you will find that the unions now often act as conservative forces, by resisting reform and modernisation in the business world and in some cases they do more harm than good to Danish workers.

Even so, there is a deep-rooted, if not sympathy, then at least tolerance of union activities in Denmark. There are fewer strikes nowadays than there used to be but it is quite likely that you at some stage will suddenly find that for a period buses don't run when the drivers are out on strike, ships don't sail, the daycare centre is closed while personnel meet to discuss union matters, papers don't come out or hospitals are slowed down while nurses strike for better pay.

The peculiar thing is the public reaction to all these inconveniences, which is generally one of patience and understanding. The otherwise often short-tempered Danes find labour conflicts all right, it is an age-old tradition in Danish society and one they are willing to accept some loss of production to preserve.

In line with the humanitarian tradition, workers enjoy a number of rights, including the right to strike. (Photo: Jens Henriksen)

Apart from occasional disputes and wildcat conflicts, Danish industrial relations are highly structured and well organised. Some modern union leaders have adopted the corporatist approach which sees the benefits in maintaining high productivity in order to promote job security. Within this system, management, labour and government all play a role in keeping labour relations on an even keel in Denmark.

Major agreements on pay and conditions are negotiated regularly through collective bargaining between unions and employers. Usually the outcome falls within government and chief macro-economist guidelines. Most Danish employees are members of one union or another, in some but not all jobs, union membership is compulsory.

Joining a union qualifies you for unemployment benefits, which are higher than ordinary welfare and as a union member you are also entitled to sabbatical leave and early retirement. Union contributions are quite high but even then these funds only cover about 20% of the eligible benefits, the rest is granted by public revenue.

INTERNATIONAL HUMANITARIANISM

As we have seen, Danish society is packed with paradoxes. There is a general uniformity and peer pressure not to be too different and yet there is a rebellious attitude to speak out and to question authority. Every person has his or her own set of opinions on things, few truths are accepted as universal. If someone comes forward and claims that tobacco smoking is bad for your health, the next day some doctor will appear in public claiming to document that smoking is no danger to your heath, that it actually benefits you by relaxing you, and he will then proceed to form a society campaigning for smokers' rights. (It is hard to believe but I have actually watched that happen.)

The Danes consider some values universal to all mankind and to the extent where they are prepared to go out into the world and promote them. Things like personal freedom, equality and democracy are issues the Danes support throughout the world. The pressure put on China to improve its human rights record is just one example. Denmark spends US$1.5 billion yearly on foreign aid to about 21 selected countries with very low GNPs. Much of this is tied to conditions regarding the recipient's willingness to promote democracy and fight corruption.

Whereas some may see Denmark as an example of liberalism and humanitarianism running out of control, to many Danes it is this aspect of their culture that they are most proud of. Although many may voice an uneasiness with certain aspects of the welfare system or the administration of law and order, they are mostly firm in their belief that whatever problems Denmark has, other countries have in far greater measure. For the newcomer, settling in to life in Denmark can be difficult unless you are prepared to accept that this is a society which is largely built on this humanitarian tradition and one that is unlikely to forsake these principles in the foreseeable future.

Chapter Five

SETTLING IN

So, it may be because of Denmark's humanitarian traditions – or perhaps in spite of them – that you have decided to live in the country. Denmark might appear a neat and affable country at first glance, and in many ways it is. If you arrive during one of the three summer months and tour around a bit, staying for a short while in different places, you will be impressed. If you come to settle in on some dark November day and want to find a home and a job and a group of friends, be prepared for some degree of hardship. Although the combination of the harsh climate and Danish character can be the cause of some initial difficulties, the rewards for persevering can be rich. When you have encountered adversity and prevailed, the experience is often all the more rewarding – keep telling yourself this, it will help you overcome some of the initial culture shock you will encounter.

SETTING UP RESIDENCE

First of all, there are some practicalities that you have to attend to. If you happen to be an asylum-seeker or have already obtained your refugee status, once you pass the examinations by the not-always-so-friendly police department and immigration authorities there will be scores of cordial helpers to take care of you. Within the Department of Refugees, the Red Cross and others involved with settling refugees, you have access to all the information and advice you are going to need.

It's a slightly different story if you are moving to Denmark to work or because you have decided to make a lifestyle change. First of all you must make sure your immigration status is in order. If you are on a three-month visa you must apply at least two weeks before expiry to have it extended. You apply to *Direktoratet for Udlændinge* (the Department for Aliens) within the Ministry of the Interior. If you obtain resident status, according to the different criteria described in Chapter One, the first thing the authorities will give you is a *personnummer*, a personal code number issued by *Folkeregistret*, the National Register. The National Register office is part of the municipal administration and is quite important to you, this is where you must register by law if you change address and your right to vote and to social benefits is dependent on which municipal office you are connected to.

Once you are issued with a personal code number (CPR) the authorities really have you on record. All your records are filed under this number and your passport now becomes obsolete. You use this number every time you apply to the authorities, file your tax return, go to the doctor, borrow books at the library or open a bank account.

Your whole life story is somewhere in the computer under this access code. The number consists of your birthday in six digits followed by four more digits, of which the last digit is an even number for females and odd for males.

Although you are issued a certificate together with the number, this does not carry your photograph and, amazingly enough, it is seldom required for identification. Be aware that since you do not have a proper ID card in Denmark the number can easily be misused fraudulently by others and you should keep it secret. Even immigrants from the EU must apply for the CPR number. Special rules apply to foreign experts on three-year contracts or less. For instance, they only pay 25% (not 50%–60%) income tax. Bring forms from home to show that you are entitled to medical insurance and child benefits. For 15,000–20,000 kroner, a private consultant will do all this for you.

A PLACE TO LIVE

Finding temporary accommodation in Denmark without any support is tough. By support, I mean assistance from either public authorities or private companies with plenty of resources. Once you are resident you can settle in any part of the country you like and you are always free to move. By law, all families in Denmark have a right to a place to live and the municipal administration will appoint a place for you in council housing if you are unable to take care of yourself. Likewise, if you have been moved to Denmark by an employer or an embassy, your employer will most likely help you find suitable lodgings. If this is the case, you have no real worries except how many bedrooms you can get within your allowance, what the view is like or how big the garden is going to be.

For everybody in between these two extremes life is a little tougher. Surveys have shown that about half of all tenants receive public rent support. That means that those who do not qualify for support are at a disadvantage. And since rents are controlled and generally kept artificially low, there is a perennial shortage of rental accommodation, especially around Copenhagen but also in other major towns like Århus, Ålborg and Odense, which have many tertiary educational institutions attracting older students.

Often, large, attractive apartments in Copenhagen are rented out way below market price and there is a rent control board which rigorously guards against any increases in rent, so these places never make it onto the open market. It is an outdated system which benefits those with connections, who through the grape-vine get the news and move into these apartments as soon as they are vacated, often subletting to avoid formulating a new contract. Newcomers rarely have a chance of renting here.

The system also tends to discourage new developments of private housing and for some years construction has been almost at a standstill. An incredible 40% of all housing is pre-World War II and much of it is in need of renovation. Try to look elsewhere for a home.

Home Ownership

Municipal housing departments may be of some help, even if you do not qualify for rental support but otherwise you have to rely on commercial estate agents or the newspapers. Since the rental market is so tightly controlled, many Danes prefer to buy their home, in fact today there are more owners than tenants (ratio: 55/45). About 60% of Danish families stay in a so-called *parcelhus,* which is a bungalow with a garden. Usually they own it themselves. Another 10% live on larger farming estates, only 30% live in apartment blocks.

As a foreigner you may not be too keen on owning your own home. Ownership carries responsibilities concerning maintenance, taxation and insurance and buying and selling is very costly in estate agent's and lawyer's fees. In addition, the way house prices have moved during the last 15 years or so has meant that property has not been a particularly good investment. The market bottomed out in 1996 and has since recovered some, but home ownership as an investment is not advisable unless you plan to stay for at least five years in the same place.

When my family and I made the decision to move to Denmark, we bought a home there by fax, on just a hunch and a piece of advice from a friend in the same estate. We had never seen the house and didn't even know exactly where the town was, but we thought that if some people could live there so could we. The deciding factor for us at the time was that the place was somewhere near where much of our family lived.

I presume few people are ready to do something like that and economically it was a poor move, as similar houses still today trade for less than we paid three years ago! However, since we had three small children we were anxious to have a place ready for us by the time we arrived in the country and luckily the estate turned out to be a great place to live.

If you do buy, property prices in Denmark are still quite low compared to major European cities. For less than US$100,000 you can get a decent apartment in Copenhagen or a small house in the country, for double that you can move into a fancy villa within commuting distance of the capital.

Renting

If you rent, expect to pay about US$400–500 for a room and US$800–1,000 for an apartment or a small house, obviously depending on location and facilities. Like everywhere else you enter into a tenancy agreement with the landlord, usually paying two or three times the monthly rental as a deposit.

You will not be required to produce references from previous contacts and as a tenant you are well protected by legislation against eviction and rent increases. When you move out however, be aware that the Danes are very strict regarding quality and maintenance of the premises, the landlord will deduct the cost of any repair or paint job he feels is necessary from your deposit and there is little you will be able to do about that.

The Commune Tradition

Traditionally, the Danes organise themselves in very small units – the so called family nucleus, which consists of husband, wife and one, two or three children, rarely more. Many Danes even stay alone, statistics show that 30% of households are only one person, 65% are two to five persons and only 5% are six or more, indicating that very few couples have more than three children or have parents staying with them. Furthermore, a number of those large families that do turn up in the statistics are likely to be immigrants.

So, the norm is for small Danish families to live in their own house, isolated from each other by hedges and fences. But where there is a rule there is also an exception to the rule and for a number of years many young Danes experimented with ways to break down this unsociable and awkward pattern. They would get together and start 'hippy' style communes with a few or many couples and young families living together and sharing everything. In the 1990s this lifestyle is no longer in fashion, although pockets remain, most notably the notorious Christiania Village, which is an enclave near the centre of Copenhagen that has been occupied by squatters for many years. In most other places police would have moved in to clear the area but not in humanitarian Denmark. Although reputedly a centre for drug trafficking and organised crime, Christiania enjoys strong political support among left-wing parties, and many of the inhabitants do make an effort to support themselves through small business ventures, while attempting to build up a different, more caring, congenial and sociable society.

Andelsboliger

A leftover from this tradition, although a slightly different concept, are the *andelsboliger* in Denmark. This is an option for finding a place to live that you ought to consider as a newcomer. An *andelsbolig* means a share-home and it is a type of home where you own a share of a larger estate, it can either be an apartment block or a development with semi-detached, grounded houses. You are supposed to buy a share and become a part owner but in many estates you can also rent units for shorter or longer terms.

Many houses are quite small, limited by regulations to 96 square metres of living space, but if you look around you can find some larger than that. As a shareholder you are responsible for maintenance of the whole estate but you do this together with your neighbours and often these meetings become social events where you meet your friends, catch up on the local gossip and do the chores along the way. Most estates have a community house where meals are cooked for everybody on certain days, although arrangements obviously vary from place to place.

My own family stays in such a development, we own our unit as a share of the whole estate with 15 houses. All are occupied with couples of about our own age and all households have children, from one to four per house and from babies to teenagers. We take turns cooking supper and gather Mondays to Thursdays outside school holidays for meals at the community house where we can also arrange games and parties. We have regular meetings and an annual general meeting where we discuss matters of common concern, finances, estate maintenance and future activities.

We have a park-like ground around the place with children's playgrounds and a small soccer field. My wife and I have tried to introduce hired help to keep the place up but our neighbours insist on doing everything themselves. So as a result, we have the office manager for the Economic Department in the municipality staying here and when he is not handling the one and a half billion dollar budget, he is out mowing the community lawn. His wife is a doctor in private practice who in the meantime does the laundry – with three young children they have a lot of laundry! The surgeon in the other house is out painting window frames, the architect down the lane is changing the oil in his car and his neighbour, the county's chief biologist is across in the community house scrubbing down the toilet. It may sound crazy but that is the way the Danes want it.

Is there an explanation to this madness – to why these bright and highly educated people insist on washing floors and shovelling snow when there are scores of low-skilled people in the country with nothing to do? The Danes pride themselves on being independent and self-reliable, they value craftsmanship and manual work – mentally they still have their roots back in the old farming community where everybody took care of his own place. Also, they cannot always afford to get help; salaries for skilled jobs are not very high considering the level of taxation. Even if both adults in the family work there is no surplus to pay employees, even if there was, the Danes would rather do the manual work themselves and save the money for a family party or a vacation abroad.

Moving In

Actually, the price of labour has been stagnant for some time in Denmark and is slowly adjusting, relatively, to international levels, so it is not exceedingly expensive to get somebody to help you, for instance, when you move into your new home. Still, many Danes

Residents of an andelsbolig – a community housing concept popular in Denmark and an ideal way of easing into Danish society.

prefer to move themselves in the prevailing national 'Do It Yourself' spirit. People simply rent a truck complete with packing boxes and move house with the help of a few friends.

I must say that the D.I.Y. thing is one aspect of living in Denmark that will quickly give you an inferiority complex, unless you happen to be an expert carpenter, bricklayer, electrician, car mechanic, computer technician, gardener and cook all rolled into one. I for one am certainly none of the above and there were times, during the first few months in the country, when I started wondering whether I was the only person in the country who could not quickly install a new staircase in the house and lay tiles across the front garden. All my new neighbours certainly knew how do those kinds of things, most of them had tool rooms that would match many a professional workman. I had an old cardboard box containing a hammer, a pair of pliers, a piece of electric wire, a roll of tape and a few nails, only slightly used.

The result of all this was that we used professionals to do the handy-work around the house for us, much to the amazement of our neighbours – and to the people we hired as well for that matter. They were not used to doing jobs in private homes, only for private and public companies and institutions where the expense can be deducted as a business cost. I guess I could have managed to install the new stereo we had to buy, as the old one was full of fungus coming from the tropics, but I preferred to take care of the kids while somebody from the dealer's office had it mounted and connected up.

Only one person turned up on the day to do the job; he drove the van, struggled with boxes and tools and wires and a ladder and mounted the speakers all by himself. The same thing happened when we ordered a washing machine, a dishwasher, additional furniture, or had carpentry work done or the windows cleaned – never more than one man turned up at a time. It puzzled me, because not only was it a lonely job for the single person, but also I had heard about all the unemployment in Denmark among young people. Why didn't a young kid tag along with each of these truly quick and competent workmen? That way they could not only help and keep each other company, the assistant could also act as an apprentice and pick up the tricks of the trade along the way. With 900,000 people between 16 and 66 on social benefits of some kind, finding candidates ought not to be a problem. I could not figure out, and I still cannot, why an intelligent people like the Danes have one group of people working extremely hard to support another group, equally large, doing absolutely nothing.

UTILITIES

Once you have registered your new address with the national register you will also start to receive mail, but it is a good idea to find out the location of your nearest post office and make sure they know where to bring your letters. Not all homes have prepared mailboxes and you might have to put up your own, which you then take along with you when you move (funny as it may sound). As with everything else in Denmark, there are strict rules concerning mailboxes, they have to meet certain criteria regarding dimensions and location, but if you buy an approved model in the local hardware store and ask the mailman where to fix it, you should be all right.

Electricity will already be connected up to your new home but make sure that a reading of the meter is done and agreed on before you move in so that you do not end up paying for somebody else's consumption.

You will usually have to wait one to three weeks before a phone line can be connected, depending on installations already in place. Once you have your phone, things are so much easier of course, the phone book alone is a treasure house of information in any country, even if you do not know the language. The listings in the yellow-pages are often illustrated with pictures and you can guess a lot of the words: if in doubt about a number call 118 and ask for information. Phoning in Denmark is a bit expensive compared to other countries. Rental is about US$140 per year, you supply your own apparatus. Overseas calls are also expensive. New call-back services are available and with liberalisation of the telecommunications market, many mobile phone providers are now setting shop. Ask around for rates and conditions. This business is a jungle, even for the locals.

In general, Denmark is quite an expensive place to be. A European Union survey in 1995 comparing expatriate living standards in European cities found Copenhagen to be the most expensive of them all. With Brussels fixed at 100, Copenhagen had an overall cost of living index of 120, Paris was second at 113, next Helsinki at 109 and Stockholm with 103. At the bottom of the scale was Athens at 80. Transport, health care and restaurants are especially expensive in Copenhagen, housing on the other hand is relatively cheap.

Keeping Warm

One final thing to consider in your home is the heating – and you are going to need it! Bungalows in the suburbs often have their own oil-furnace, in other places there is central heating, with a hot water supply piped in from a nearby power station burning coal, oil or natural gas. Thanks to fairly recent hydrocarbon production facilities being installed offshore in the North Sea, Denmark is self sufficient in oil and gas. Some coal is still imported and the modern power stations have multipurpose furnaces which can run on anything, including wood-chippings and straw and grain. Electric stoves for heating are rare in Danish homes and expensive to run and air-conditioning is only installed in selected food stores and restaurants.

It seems to me that this is one aspect that is often overlooked when comparisons are made between standards of living in countries north and south – the monetary expense which a severe climate imposes. In Denmark it costs between 1,000 and 2,000 dollars per year to heat a home, depending on the size of the place and fuel efficiency. On top of that comes cold weather clothes and footwear for the people and excessive wear and tear on buildings, cars and equipment. These are all factors that beef up the GNP of northern countries on paper but in actual fact they do very little to enhance the quality of life.

In Denmark your utility consumption is not monitored and calculated each month, often only once or twice a year. Your payments are then averaged out on a monthly basis which means that you pay the same in heating on a hot summer month as you do during the coldest winter period! That makes it difficult to gauge and reduce your consumption, but it is all part of the Danish 'pocket-money' mentality, few people are prepared to save up money during fat times and spend less during lean, the Danes prefer each month and each year to be just like all the other ones.

FINDING THE REAL DENMARK

There is this old joke of a British couple who visited the United States and landed in New York. Naturally very interesting but not really 'America.' They drove down to Texas, west to Las Vegas and then on to Los Angeles and up to Seattle, all very exciting but it was not 'America.' When they finally found the America they had expected, they realised that they had come to Alberta, Canada.

So the moral is, maybe it is not the country that is wrong, it could be your own expectations. If you just wander down Vesterbro or Nørrebro in Copenhagen and think that this is Denmark, you might be slightly shocked. The clean, well ordered streets of your expectations may be hard to find and the reality is something closer to what you will see in most big cities.

People you see are often poorly dressed, many shuffle hopelessly along with a plastic bag full of beer bottles in one hand. If you do come across a smartly dressed individual, he or she will most likely be a tourist. Is that the Denmark you expected?

Of course it isn't, and in reality there is another Denmark, in fact there are several. Go north along the coast, away a bit from the city, up into the Whisky-belt, as this section is called, and you will see where the successful people of Denmark hang out and the only enclave in the nation where you can still sense an atmosphere of affluence, even luxury at times. But then, it is not really 'Denmark' is it?

The Danish Home

I think that to find the true Denmark you have to go into the Danish home. The Danes are great homemakers, even young students and working-class people collect neat furniture in modern styles made out of steel and light coloured woods, like oak and pine. On the walls are carefully spotted posters and paintings, all selected and displayed with the greatest artistic consideration. Lighting, souvenirs, even practical appliances are carefully chosen to match aesthetically. The mandatory bookshelf is loaded with philosophical works and some of the greatest novels ever written, especially so in middle-class homes.

Often furniture and antique items are carefully preserved and handed down through the generations. This way middle-aged peoples' homes are often a more or less tasteful combination of old family heirlooms and modern designs.

Out of this traditional appreciation of craftsmanship and art has grown a Danish interest in design work and quality finish in product development. It is a national fascination which is reflected in Danish industrial production and exports and certainly in almost every home you will ever enter.

To keep up this standard, the average Dane spends a lot of time cleaning and maintaining the home. You may not see a lot of activity on Danish roads and towns after 6:00 p.m. when the rush hour traffic comes to an abrupt halt. That is when everybody is home eating and most will not be going out again that day, preferring to occupy themselves inside their own homes.

The city may look rundown but inside many of the apartments are little wonders of cleanliness and neatness. And when you go through a suburban neighbourhood take a look at the houses – they look as neat outside as they surely are inside. Hedges are cut, lawns are mowed, trees are pruned. Danes take the long view, they will go about planting trees that they realise they will never see fully grown, just to keep up the place. Much of this work is done by elderly people, by themselves and without any help from family or servants.

The Danes take great pride in their homes and appreciate craftsmanship in the furnishings they choose. Many people spend time browsing the antique stores looking for an addition to their home's decor. (Photo: Danish Tourist Board)

GETTING AROUND

The Danes cherish their homes but not necessarily their cars. You may have somebody living in a beautifully maintained villa with a large garden and when he drives to town it will be in a ten-year-old small Toyota. It is the opposite situation to Asia or the United States, where the guy in the Mercedes or the Lincoln might live in a small apartment – his love of quality motoring or a desire to show off his perceived success to his business clients compelling him to buy a flashy car above his budget.

In Denmark a showy car is regarded as slightly tasteless, even vulgar. In general, conspicuous consumption is frowned at in most quarters. Why pay hundreds of thousands dollars for a car when a cheap one will do? Haven't you heard that people are starving around the world? Don't you realise than one billion people live on less than a dollar a day? Rather than successful, a flashy car can make you feel like a fool in Denmark, and the same goes for that gold Rolex watch and designer dress. Instead of top of the heap you will be regarded by most Danes as a snob, or even worse, a parasite, exploiting the poor and the Third World. Of course it may influence their judgement that very few Danes can afford such luxury items themselves.

Nevertheless, although the cars on the roads are mostly small models and many are very old, Danes drive more and more. There are 1.6 million private cars on the road accounting for 74% of all personal transport with buses (12%), two-wheelers (7%) and trains (6%) making up most of the rest. Petrol prices are among the lowest in Europe and although registration taxes are high you can still get a decent 1800cc, medium-range European or Japanese car for about US$30,000, which seems to be many middle-class people's car budget. Diesel cars are becoming quite popular, many Danish taxis for instance are diesel engine Mercedes, which will drive ten times around the world and still run like new.

It is fairly safe to buy a second (or third) hand car in Denmark, consumers are well protected against unscrupulous dealers. If you have a no-claim bonus from your previous insurance, make sure you get a letter of reference and get it transferred to your new policy, you can save a lot of money that way. Road tax varies according to the weight of the car, I pay 770 dollars per year for a 1,325 kilogram four-door saloon, comprehensive insurance is 800 dollars per year.

Driving in Denmark is easy and parking is reasonably hassle free, even in downtown Copenhagen you can find places with unlimited free parking along the back streets, if you are prepared to walk a bit to the centre. Remember that you must have a plastic disc displayed in your front window showing the time you left your car. Under the parking sign which is blue with a large, white 'P' a time limit will be stated, often "1 time" or one hour. Be back before then or it will cost you 400 kroner. Speed limits are 50 kilometres per hour in towns, 80 on highways and 110 on motorways but few people pay any attention to those and you will be honked off the road for road-

Getting around in Denmark, whether by public or private transport, is a relatively hassle free affair. Roads are rarely congested and parking is usually easy to find, even in the cities. (Photo: Jens Henriksen)

hogging if you try to abide by them. You have to make a choice between incurring the wrath of your fellow motorists and that of the traffic police. The tourist information office has free traffic information and road maps available in English and other languages.

The bicycle is still popular in Denmark. It is amazing, even on winter days, to see people propel themselves forward across the icy surface and through the sleet and wet snow. The Danes may not be very courteous to each other, but they are a tough bunch. And on some warm summer day, riding a bicycle is obviously the only way to go around Denmark. It is a bit dangerous however, more cyclists (about 80) are killed each year in Denmark than in any other European country per capita.

If you are careful on your bicycle you actually don't really need a car in Denmark, especially if you are there on your own. For longer journeys, public transport is comfortable and most places are covered, although it is a bit expensive if you are a whole family travelling. The cheapest bus/train fare in the cities is $US1.70 in Copenhagen and $US2.00 in Århus, but then the ticket is good for respectively one and two hours and you can change buses/trains within this period – there are different additional surcharges if you go outside the city limit. The regional trains and many buses and ferries are operated by the state monopoly, DSB.

SPENDING MONEY

Shopping for the stuff you need is easy in Denmark. There are plenty of well stocked shops everywhere, although they mostly seem to carry the same products and even exactly the same brands. For variety you have to look, in the bigger towns, for specialist shops.

Once you get a mailbox you can be sure that within a few days it will be full of brochures, leaflets and catalogues distributed for free by the big chainstores and mail order businesses. To most people this is just junk-mail and you can actually apply for an official sticker at your local post office saying, "No advertising mail, thank you," but as a newcomer you might benefit and certainly you can make some bargain purchases in the big stores if you go by the junk-mail. Most Danes are bargain hunters and discounted merchandise is snapped up everywhere. Quality products are harder to find and you might be better off buying your clothes and household items abroad if you have the opportunity.

As stated, generally the cost of living in Denmark is quite high. In spite of this, many imported consumer items have come down dramatically in price in recent years, particularly those from the newer trading regions in Asia.

To be able to shop at the big discount warehouse you almost certainly will need a car. This fact has so disturbed the Danish government that now no more building permits will be granted to new super stores outside the cities. This is partly due to environmental concerns (burning of petrol) and partly to protect the local shops, frequented mainly by poor, single or older people without cars.

There is a good network of local shops in Danish towns, many of the grocery shops and the convenience stores are run by immigrants, who don't mind working the long hours and have large families to help them out. Every town will also have at least one bakery, and thank goodness for that – Danish cakes and pastries are delicious!

BANKS

Another 'shop' that each street and each town has is a bank. Recently some banks have been closing branches but there are still plenty left. The two major banks, Den Danske Bank and Unibank, have been losing money for a few years and have increased charges to prevent further losses and staff cuts. Money was lost due to poor management decisions and huge defaults by a few corrupt corporate clients but the small customers have to cover the losses. Therefore, general banking has become expensive in Denmark and there are charges for almost all services commonly provided free of charge in other countries – you are even charged a fee for asking what your bank balance is.

It does pay to shop around for a good banking connection, as some of the smaller banks have become much more competitive than the two big ones. Many of the everyday transactions are done in Denmark by plastic cards just like everywhere else. In Denmark the banks cooperate to issue a *Dan-kort*, which is a handy little cash card with your picture on it, that for an extra fee can also be used as a Visa card. With the *Dan-kort* you can of course also make withdrawals from the cash dispensers but for some reason Danish machines do not accept deposits in check or in cash like machines in other countries do. So you still find yourself queuing up in Danish banks quite a lot – not to withdraw funds but to deposit them!

Transferring money in and out of Denmark has become very quick and easy and there are few restrictions on amounts and currencies. There is a local stock market that you can play if you feel like it but you should be aware of capital gains taxes that apply if you frequently buy and sell shares.

Getting a good return on your investments is difficult these years with volatile stock prices and the historically low interest rates. Many private and institutional investors stick to bonds issued by building societies and by the government always keen to finance the enormous public debt. This way you can get decent returns of 4-5% p.a. depending on the issue. On top of that the Danish Krone is pegged to the EURO within a 2.25% band and has traditionally been fairly strong on international currency markets. That is because even though the Danish public sector has a serious debt problem, it is even worse in other countries, including former European powerhouse Germany.

SALARIES AND TAXES

Saving money is not always easy in Denmark and it is especially hard to save on a salary, the people who make it big in Denmark are the few people who successfully start their own businesses. For lower paid employees and people on benefits there is a strong disincentive to save, as this means that they will get less from the state.

In real terms salaries have been fairly stable since 1975, with that year as baseline, white collar employees are today paid on an unchanged index of 100. Manual workers have enjoyed a slight increase to 110, public employees have even declined to 85. Nevertheless, what you do and the money you make is important to Danes, as it is to people everywhere. In fact, when Danes ask you about your occupation they will ask the equivalent to, "What are you?" or, "What is your father?" meaning what does your father do for a living, this way your job is equivalent to your very existence.

Money is transferred through trade union manipulation, legislation and taxation from the privileged and well educated to the lower skilled. This way salaries and incomes end up remarkably uniform, I cannot think of another place with such uniformity of earnings across the board. Take a look at this list which was published in a Danish monthly as a career guide for 1995.

Job	Wage/mth (DKK)	US Dollars
Maid	17,670	2,524
Waiter	18,516	2,645
Cook	21,636	3,091
Cashier	13,848	1,978
Sales person	15,270	2,181
Construction worker	14,652	2,093
Taxi driver	15,432	2,204
Truck driver	20,286	2,898
Journalist	25,806	3,686
Editor	33,258	4,751
Computer programmer	23,934	3,419
Flight attendant	23,928	3,418
Pilot	36,978	5,282
Painter	19,812	2,830
Teacher	20,562	2,937
Nurse	18,090	2,584
Doctor	31,098	4,442

Lawyer	20,910	3,485
Lawyer's secretary	18,684	3,114
High court judge	53,088	8,848
Police officer	17,562	2,927
Member of parliament	28,508	4,751

As you can see, Danish salaries are remarkable similar to each other with little regard to profession or level of responsibility. The bottom income tax rate is 50% although there are some local variations depending on municipal requirements. On top of that comes 25% value added tax (VAT) in the shops when you spend what is left. There is a US$5000 per annum tax allowance per person, but it still means that lower paid part-timers pay tax on income that they cannot exist on, then have to appeal to the state for support.

And the much talked about social benefits, how high are they actually? Well, here are some of the benefits available and their current rates (2003).

Benefit	**Monthly Payment (DKK)**	**US Dollars**
Unemployment	13,498	1,708
Disabled pension	13,503	1,709
Single parent	10,859	1,374
Social welfare (single)	8,172	1,034
Early retirement	10,277	1,301
Old age pension	9,064	1,147
Student grant	4,379	554

Most of these benefits cannot be negotiated, but additional payments are given to recipients of social welfare: supplemental child support, rent support, free child care, moving expenses etc. In fact, there are documented cases where a single mother would make less money if she took a job.

Talking about jobs, in the next chapter we take a look at the employment situation and the working environment in Denmark.

— Chapter Six —

WORKING (AND NOT WORKING) LIFE

THE TRUE UNEMPLOYMENT

It has been said that statistics are like a bikini – they reveal a lot but hide the most important parts. That is certainly true when you look at the statistics concerning working life in Denmark.

Before we moved to Denmark my wife and I were repeatedly told that life there would be hard for us, that it was not easy to settle in, that it was difficult to find employment. I wasn't too worried though, I had managed and succeeded abroad in different careers – how could I not succeed in my home country where I was a citizen, where I spoke the language and with all the experience I now had? Anyway, I wasn't even looking for a job, I just wanted to continue doing what I had done for years – take pictures and write. My wife had her own company in the ladies fashion wear business – how could we possibly fail? However, it did make an impression on me that even my mother told me to be careful, to expect difficult times; she who was such a hard-working and successful person herself and who had always had a refreshing 'can-do' attitude to life.

Well, we didn't fail but it was tougher settling in than I had expected, in spite of us and our families being well established and connected. It is true, working life in Denmark is demanding and is tougher still for somebody arriving without connections or without being able to speak the language. Employment is hard to find and new business ventures are difficult to get off the ground. Not impossible, just more difficult than in places like East Asia and the United States, where there is an underlying sense of optimism and a tradition of individual ambition and entrepreneurship. I had always believed that if you really want to, you can always find work but for the first time I have met in Denmark people who genuinely want to work but who cannot do so.

And when you study the statistics, remember, they do not reveal the most important areas! Take the unemployment statistics. A student of the Danish society will look in the paper and find out that the rate of unemployment is currently 8%. It must be added that I am of the generation now labelled with the tag 'baby-boomers.' When I dropped out of college and went to work abroad in 1973 the unemployment rate was 1.5%, it had been low since I could walk and talk and we never thought that it would get any different. If you wouldn't or couldn't do anything else, you could always go out and get a job.

But 8% unemployment is not so bad, the newcomer to Denmark will say, all I have to do is be among the other 92% and I will be alright. But it doesn't work that way. Consider a survey on the Danish employment structure published in 1993 by a professor at the Odense University, J. H. Petersen.

Petersen found that at the time of the survey 1,918,000 people were working full time in Denmark. What about all the others? 325,000 were unemployed, that is fine, this is the number that is usually published. But on top of that 260,000 people were receiving early retirement benefits; 88,000 were included in another early retirement scheme; no less than 500,000 received social welfare benefits, disablement pensions, illness or maternity payments; 30,000 received a state pension; and another 713,000 received the usual old age pension that all citizens are entitled to. What do you get when you add that up? 1,916,000 people – half the adult population supporting the other half.

The numbers have changed a bit since then. After 1995 the economy finally regained some of its competitiveness and there was an increase in jobs available. So unemployment has come down but that is partly because another scheme has been introduced, a system of sabbatical leave where currently (1997) 67,000 people are on state supported activities, like education, baby-sitting or travel. During the leave they receive 70–80% of the unemployment benefit, depending on the activity they are involved in.

Calculated this way the unemployment rate is much higher than the official figures suggest. Including organisations mainly sponsored by the state (like the state television and the Church) public services in Denmark employ some 955,000 people, this number has grown by 350,000 since 1970 and now accounts for approximately half the workforce.

Subcontracted work projects are initiated by the state and subsidies are given to private projects also to create jobs. Many individuals registered as independent business people and barely scraping by, would in fact, much rather take a job if one was available. The real employment opportunities for new people striking out in Denmark do not total 92%, but the other way around – the de facto employment rate is more likely 8%! These are the realities that the newcomer trying to settle in will have to face.

FARMING THE DANISH WAY

Denmark used to be mainly an agricultural country. Even 50 years ago, shortly after the Second World War, as much as 40% of the population were working in the farming sector. By 1970 that had declined to 11% and today the number is 4.4%. That doesn't mean that production has decreased accordingly – just the opposite, within the last 30 years farming production has more than tripled. Output has now increased to the point where huge surpluses of farming produce are accumulated. There are enormous stockpiles of food stashed away within the European Union: 907,000 tons of grain and 46,000 tons of beef at this moment, the storage costs alone are a major burden to the Union.

My family owns a small house near the west coast of Jutland and we go there once in a while to relax during vacations. It is close to the beach in a rural countryside, different from our everyday city and suburban surroundings. Nearby is a farm, it is run by one man, the farmer is our friend and I often take my kids down to his place to let them look at the animals and see what farming work is like.

Today the farm is mainly a dairy farm, a few years back the farmer produced pigs but he switched to cows, something he might regret today as pig farming these days generally pays better money. He has about 60 cows that he milks and as many calves that he rears for meat production. He produces his own feed on vast fields surrounding the place planted with grain, hay and beets. The amazing thing is that this one man does all the work himself. He works in the fields, feeds and milks and cleans the cattle, he is his own mechanic and carpenter. He has three sons, but they are usually too busy going to school or doing other work to help him. In spite of a huge daily output he doesn't make that much money, the interest and depreciation on the farm and all the necessary machinery making this productivity possible eat up most of his revenue. In fact his wife has to work as a nurse in a nearby town so they can make ends meet.

All the cattle on the farm are kept indoors year round as the farmer does not have the resources to lead them to and from the fields everyday for milking. He struggles from dusk to dawn to get the work done without any outside help, while around the local region thousands of able young men are drawing unemployment benefits. He is penalised with fines if he produces more milk than his quota allows and a new system recently introduced, forces him to leave parts of his land untended. He can only survive because of a state regulated system that forces the consumer to pay above world market prices for his milk and meat. His meat is far more expensive and of far inferior quality to free ranging beef from Australia or America – this of course few Danes are aware of, as this beef cannot be imported into Europe, so the Danes happily think they produce the best farming products in the world!

It must be said that in these times of gross over production of traditional food stuffs, some Danish farmers have shown a lot of innovation in finding alternative niches. Some rear racehorses, ostriches or turkeys or new, exotic produce, others farm mink for fur production. Not all farmers struggle against bankruptcy. Subsidies keep rising and on an average the state subsidy to each farm in Denmark amounts to over US$30,000.

Agriculture and the European Union

So why does the public allow this state of affairs? Why do people accept that their money is being spent to keep one occupation going under these conditions? Well, changing things in Denmark is not an easy process. For one thing, most policies today are tied in closely with common policies within the European Union. When Denmark became a member in 1972 the EEC, as it was then called, was mostly an economic block but gradually integration has taken place and today most domestic legislation has to be carefully worded to correlate with EU regulations. In effect, very few major decisions can be taken unilaterally by Denmark, especially those relating to farming policy which is one of the most important building blocks of European cooperation.

Near our home in the suburbs are some fields, on our first summer there one was planted with barley, a grain resembling wheat. Come harvest time I took our smallest son across as soon as they rolled out the combiner and the tractors. The sun was shining from a clear blue sky, this was a significant day, when the crop of the year was recovered and brought home, I was sharing this special moment with the next generation.

The farmer piled up the grain on a huge tarpaulin awaiting further transport and I went across to have a friendly chat with him. "What a magnificent harvest of grain," I said, "you have had a good year, haven't you?" "Yes," said the farmer wryly, "I guess I had better take that damned stuff in before it rots, now they are probably going to burn it!" What happened to the joy of producing great food for all mankind, the thrill of a successfully completed harvest time? Maybe my notion of country life is somewhat romantic, maybe it was never like that, or maybe the agricultural policy of the EU has developed this cynical attitude in the farmer. At that time there was talk about using the excess grain production for fuel in electric power stations.

So as the Danish rural identity slowly fades, the Danes now look to other areas for employment. Again, the European Union tends to be shaping the future career paths of the Danish workers and from this influence a new working identity is being forged.

THE GAINFULLY EMPLOYED

In Denmark most people work in service industries. Some 68% of the working population are engaged in private or public services of some sort. Most of the others work in manufacturing, and in building and construction.

In Denmark, services are where the opportunities lie and this section of Danish society is slowly expanding and very gradually eating into farming and heavy industry. This is important to the newcomer to Denmark – if you are looking for a niche in the Danish workplace this is where you should start searching.

During the postwar period, when Denmark for a while had full employment, people were manufacturing all kinds of general consumer items and making a living from that. When I grew up our clothes, shoes, bicycles, radio, kitchen wear, toys, even the batteries powering our flashlight were produced domestically. Most of these items plus many new ones are now imported from the Far East at massively reduced prices.

EMPLOYMENT OPPORTUNITIES

One of the great ironies of working life in Denmark is that the working population is often really overworked. To be able to pay the high taxes necessary to support all those not working, the people in employment have to pull in a lot of money to make ends meet. It is not unusual for policemen to drive a taxi at night and for carpenters to work on a friend's house during the weekend.

It is also a fact that in spite of the 169,000 officially unemployed Danes, plus 480,000 (1999) adults on other welfare schemes, there are employers who cannot find workers. Locally, in certain regions of Denmark, there can be pockets of activity, businesses and sectors which suddenly find expanding markets for their products. They are then unable to find help if people with the right skills are not in the neighbourhood. There are strict rules protecting the unemployed, they are not obliged to travel outside the county to take work – and many claim this right and prefer to stay unemployed at home rather than move where they are needed.

Large Corporations

Some of the biggest industrial employers are located around the country, not near Copenhagen. Danfoss on the remote island of Als is one of the biggest of them all, employing 20,000 people, making cooling and heating appliances; Lego at Billund in Jutland are world renowned for their building blocks and toys and employ almost 4,300 people (plus 5,700 abroad); Grundfos at Bjerringbro produce pumping equipment with 8,600 hands; Bang and Olufsen are also in Jutland, in the town of Struer, with 3,000 people turning out television and radio sets of unique quality and design.

Mærsk Corporation is one of the largest employers in Denmark. Here workers search for oil aboard one of the company's oil exploration vessels.

Many of these companies are major exporters and contribute to the economy's enormous balance of payments receipts, totalling US$80 billion (expenditures being $80 billion and total foreign debt a modest $40 billion). Denmark is also home to some large conglomerate companies doing many things and operating in many countries. The old East Asiatic Company (mainly shipping/12,500 employees) is the country's largest exporter, followed by J. Lauritzen Holdings (mainly shipping/11,600) and FLS Industries (mainly construction materials/18,000).

Other important businesses in Denmark are insurance, finance, furniture and office supplies, power and utilities, publishing, technical consultancy, metal supplies, wood and paper and chemicals. Since exploration started in 1966 and especially in later years, with many new finds of offshore hydrocarbon deposits, oil and natural gas drilling, production and transport has become another important Danish business. Today Denmark is self sufficient in oil and a major player in the North Sea activities is the A.P. Møller/Mærsk conglomerate which is a very successful Danish shipping enterprise known worldwide, but the concern is largely family owned and the full accounts are not made public so the status of this company is somewhat cryptic.

Smaller Companies

Generally, Danish business life is characterised by many smaller firms. There are 430,000 firms registered, but of these, most (more than 300,000) are sole proprietorships with just the proprietor working. Half of all the firms have a turnover of less than US$100,000. Only 23,000 are private limited companies. About 250 companies have a yearly turnover of more than 100 million dollars, less than two percent have more than 500 employees, most of the industrial companies have less than 100 employees.

Nevertheless, many of these smaller and medium sized companies are doing quite well. This is especially so in information based industries. The main problem expressed by business executives is the accumulation of capital, which is difficult. It is also a problem in Danish society that in spite of an energetic and dynamic private sector, that is quick and skilful in seeking new ventures, growth does not always translate into jobs. Nevertheless, there are some opportunities for those who are keen to work.

FINDING A JOB

If you are eager to secure a job, there are a number of things you should do. In Denmark many people still go job hunting by reading the papers and applying for jobs advertised. Sunday editions are greatly expanded and have special sections with job openings. It is a tedious process however – circulating your CV and writing enthusiastic cover letters. One of our young family members who is just out from collage with a useful BA in language and business administration has tried this and has never received a single reply. Some of these adds are being responded to by as many as 800 applicants, sometimes twice as many. Even getting short-listed for an interview is difficult. Companies or governmental organisations often advertise when in fact they already have somebody earmarked for the job, people already in employment are often preferred, so the papers in effect provide a rotation deal for all the insiders.

A better approach is to selectively target your goals. If you have an advanced education or special qualifications you should investigate the situation in your field. You may need to apply to have your qualifications recognised in Denmark. Most major occupations have trade unions and branch organisations who can help here, and with regard to the validity of your academic qualifications, a nearby university's student advisory office should be consulted. In most jobs a reasonable command of the Danish language is a necessity and it is certainly always an advantage. Enrol in Danish classes, the language is tough but it can be learned – thousands have done it before you! Try to use your second language and your cultural background to your advantage so you have an edge over Danes applying for the same job.

107

If you have a special interest, get involved in a volunteer or a freelance capacity for a society or a small company, it may one day lead to a regular job. This was the route I took myself. I have involved myself in bird-watching activities since I was a kid, it was just a hobby but I ended up over the years doing countless bird-watching surveys and outings, took pictures, did talks, wrote articles, and one day when the Danish Ornithological Society needed an International Officer I was selected for the job.

A friend of mine did something similar. A refugee from South America, he stayed active, he explored his interest in Latin American culture, his knowledge of the Spanish language, his interest in computers and communication. He took some courses in desktop publishing and electronic media production - and he ended up doing radio and television shows for the local network.

If you have no qualifications you can try to upgrade your skills. Or you can apply for unskilled work – cleaning work and sometimes some factory or restaurant work is often available for those who are willing to do anything, anywhere, any time. The Danes prefer rooms and interior fixtures to be spotlessly clean, so if you are good at cleaning up you should never be bored! The company ISS, which does cleaning, is one of the country's biggest employers with no less than 11,000 employees. The minimum wage for adults (approx US$11 per hour) is such that you will make a reasonable living even from those kinds of jobs. These low-budget jobs may not be advertised but there are governmental job centres in all major towns where you can apply, the so-called AF-Centres – this is where the employers will go when they need casual labour.

But these days in Denmark, as well as most other places, jobs are mainly filled through networking. It is a fact of life that most people like to work and do business with people they know, like and trust. Surveys have shown that managers tend to hire and promote people who are like themselves. Supervisors prefer to take in people that they are familiar with or who are recommended to them by people they

trust. The lesson in this of course is that the newcomer should get out there and meet people and start building up a network.

As a foreigner you may never be like your potential manager but if you want to get ahead you should try to at least fit in. Observe how the Danes get along and do things. When you gain a bit of confidence don't hide in a corner, come forward and exert yourself. It is a mistake if you think you should just imitate your peers and superiors, you should be yourself and be proud of what you are and what you have done, the Danes will respect and even admire you as long as you don't boast or try to impose your views and methods on them.

EMPLOYMENT MATTERS

Hiring somebody in Denmark is a serious matter, the employer will usually be very careful that everything is done correctly because once a worker is in he may not be so easy to get rid of and the costs of employing people are high. Pay is usually slightly higher in the Copenhagen area in line with the cost of living. Allowing for the bottom rate of 50% income tax after a monthly allowance of about US$400 your starting take-home pay is typically around US$1,500 a month.

Salaries in Denmark are fixed by rigid rules and negotiating better terms or moving to another company for better conditions is very difficult, because everybody gets the same or similar wages across the board. The huge public sector has a published table of pay where each single job and each step on the promotional ladder is described and categorised. Most Danes feel very comfortable and secure with this predictable regularity, they generally don't like surprises. In 1998 a more performance based system of remuneration was introduced as a reaction to low productivity in the civil service.

In the private sector conditions are not much different. Both blue-collar and white-collar workers are highly organised and for many, membership of a union is a prerequisite for a job. Although it has come down slightly within the last decade, at 86%, Denmark still has one of the highest percentages of unionised workers in the world, only surpassed by Sweden.

So the individual is highly regulated in this society with regards to working conditions and pay. Pay is negotiated by collective bargaining, which usually consists of the workers in employment gaining a small pay rise and a half hour cut in the working week every other year.

In the Workplace

There are a number of rules in Danish workplaces regarding safety, holidays, liaison committees, insurance schemes and pension plans. Don't worry too much about these, there will be plenty of people to tell you all you need to know. Danes love rules and regulations and most likely they have them all written down in leaflets, memos and company newsletters.

Expect to work hard in your job. The Danes value quality, and to maintain a high productivity they pace themselves hard and expect others to do the same. They try to be effective every working minute, they do not believe in long breaks. At meetings they come straight to the point without any small talk. When the working day is over they abruptly cease activities and go home. If you prefer things any other way you will find little sympathy. The Danes are a very homogeneous society, values are generally shared and you will find few listeners if you want to introduce new ones. Your colleagues will not be interested in how you used to do things back home. Your best bet is to be on time, take your cue from how things are being done and follow suit.

Once you settle in, open up gradually. If you have an interest, check if it is shared. Join a company organised activity and get to know your fellow workers better. If you are good at playing soccer or table tennis or any other game, or if you have an artistic streak this will usually win you points. Don't be intimidated by the situation, like most people, Danes respect confident and self-assured people. Be friendly and helpful but don't be weak. There are cases of foreigners being discriminated against but locals, new in town and perceived to be soft and easy targets, are basically treated the same way, so colour and creed may not be the criteria.

As soon as you can, mix with your colleagues and join in the conversation. Danes naturally talk shop like everybody else but they are especially interested in fellow workers and superiors and what they are up to. Housing, cars and do-it-yourself projects are other popular topics. If you are a man among men you can never go wrong if you talk about the opposite sex – if you are a woman among women the same thing applies!

Out of Work

Once you have been a member of an unemployment fund for a minimum of one year and have been working for 26 weeks within the last three years, you are entitled to unemployment benefits should you lose your job. When you become unemployed you are into a different ball-game altogether, you are no longer taking care of yourself – you are now part of the 'other half,' the second half of the adult population in Denmark that is currently depending on the state for a living. This world is a jungle of legislation, of rules and regulations, of meetings with counsellors, of endless correspondence and very often complaints and appeals to higher authorities. Welcome to the welfare state. If you come from any other kind of society it is a peculiar and mind-boggling way of doing things.

The rules concerning welfare benefits are numerous and complicated and change by the year, sometimes by the month. Often, not even the authorities know exactly what your entitlements are. So for the latest update you must contact the nearest municipal social security office. Here is just a quick guideline to what happens if you join the ranks of the unemployed.

As an unemployed worker you are entitled to benefits covering 90% of your previous salary but there is a ceiling of approximately US$1,709 per month and you pay income tax on this. You must be available to take a job should one be offered to you within the county

The morning rush hour in Copenhagen – perhaps not as hectic as some European cities, but Copenhagen is the commercial hub of Denmark.

where you stay. You must register with the local job centre and attend meetings to discuss your situation. After 65 weeks of this, if you still have not had any employment, you will be kicked out of the unemployment fund. But do not fear, the authorities will not let that happen. The job centre representing the municipality where you live must get you a job. How do they do that? – They create one. Either by subsidising a private company position for you or, more likely, by putting you to work in a child care centre run by the municipality, or weeding the flowerbeds on one of its properties. After seven months of this you go back on benefits. You are also entitled to a variety of courses and training, including a free education, lasting up to two and a half years, instead of a job offer if you are under 50-years-old. You are also entitled to holidays and if you have small children you can apply for a six month child minding sabbatical leave.

Within this system, some chronically unemployed people receive benefits for six or even eight years, interspersed with job offers. Eventually, even they will run out of options and have to leave the unemployment fund. When this happens you now step down another notch on the Danish social ladder and receive social welfare.

STARTING YOUR OWN BUSINESS

In response to the unemployment problem in Denmark people are now encouraged to start their own businesses. Traditionally, running your own business was not a high-status activity but it is gaining wider acceptance as the Danish working environment continues to change.

You can contact your local public business adviser about what to do, there are 120 of them strategically located around the country. Call the Ministry of Trade and Industry (3392 3350) for further information. Some counties have a centre for jobs and enterprises that you can contact. I did that when I first arrived in the county of Århus and wanted to transfer my business activities from Singapore to Denmark. It proved to be fairly easy; I only visited the office once and there is a lot of help and advice to be had here if you meet the right people.

The Ministry will organise free counselling for you, where they evaluate your idea for a business and put you in contact with others who can help you get started. It is all part of a policy to support the establishment of new businesses and eventually create jobs for people. Accountants and legal advisers make themselves available for discussions – totally free of charge out of a budget with a US$4,000 ceiling made available for you by the Ministry.

While the Danish government, as we have seen, supports agriculture with heavy state subsidies, there is generally not much help given directly to private enterprises and many small companies therefore are quite lean, dynamic and internationally competitive. An exception is small businesses started up by unemployed people, who can apply for a grant to assist them during the first four years. You have to have been out of work for a minimum of five months and the grant is a monthly support equal to half the full unemployment benefit. It is not much but it will help to see you through the first few years, before your business can make a profit. You also have to submit and get approved a complete plan for your new business venture before you are entitled to the support. The scheme has been criticised by established small businesses, like shopkeepers and hairdressers, who complain that the state supported newcomers offer them unfair competition. Nevertheless, this scheme is worth looking into if you meet the criteria to qualify.

Otherwise, you register a business like you do in most other countries. There are basically two levels on which to operate. You can either become a sole proprietor where you are responsible for the business with all your personal assets or you can form a private limited company where you only risk your own and others paid up share capital. There are two kinds of private limited companies, one requiring US$30,000 capital and one requiring US$80,000. Companies not only demand a considerable start-up capital, they are also expensive to establish in legal fees and the legislation is strict concerning organisation and book-keeping. Therefore, most small firms are the sole proprietorship kind. You can register with or without a partner and there are no other requirements than to file a name, then you are issued a registration number, called the SE-number. You are now in business.

You are required to keep accounts of all transactions within the business, and you have to provide quarterly VAT statements and yearly annual accounts to the Inland Revenue Department. Very likely somebody from Told & Skat, the VAT office, will visit your premises at some stage, so make sure you are ready for it. Once you have seen to these administrative details all that remains is to go out and sell yourself and your product or service.

Chapter Seven

YOUR FAMILY IN DENMARK

CULTURE SHOCK AND YOUR CHILDREN

So, now that you are out there trying to get some work done and make ends meet, naturally you wonder how your family will fare in these new surroundings. If you don't have your family with you, you will probably be wondering whether it is a good idea to bring them to Denmark.

When my wife and I decided to move to Denmark our family, and especially our three children, were our main consideration. And in that respect Denmark has not disappointed us, it is certainly a great place to bring up children.

There were a few predicaments as we settled in. The first winter that never seemed to come to an end was not all that amusing, I pulled the kids to play-school on a sled through the snow for a while, which was good fun, but there were many other wet, cold and windy days where the darkness appeared to last forever and the kids had to stay indoors most of the time.

One of our sons didn't adapt well, his Danish wasn't good and he had problems communicating and getting along with the other kids and the new adults in his life. He grew increasingly introverted and non-constructive in his activities. Danish kids become independent at an early age, they are left on their own a lot and there seem to be many arguments and fights amongst them as they establish their roles and a hierarchy. Our son didn't know the rules of this game and he missed his 'home' in Singapore. I was gone a lot, still visiting Asia regularly, and my wife was under some strain with all the practical chores – he didn't know how to handle his new situation and was basically suffering from culture shock.

The play-school arranged for some meetings with a child psychologist. I was a bit apprehensive at first, I don't believe in doctors, they tend to make you more sick, but I went along and as it turned out the psychologist was a nice person who was focused and result-oriented, he actually helped us get out of the jam.

We had our son's language skills tested and, sure enough, he was behind his age-group in language development. So we cut out all English at home and spoke with him and read aloud to him a lot in Danish, at play-school he was given special Danish classes by a language tutor. The psychologist also told us to build up his self esteem; encourage him in the things he was good at, praise him when he did well. At the same time we should draw some clear demarcations as to what was not acceptable and enforce them. Rather than confront trouble with his peers and hope to mould him into being like the other kids we should avoid distress and accept that he was different and probably always would be. It worked and I guess much of it is universal advice.

Quality Childcare

Apart from that, our kids have been doing well here and conditions for children are outstanding in most places in Denmark. Where we stay we can walk 500 metres across an open field to a childcare centre for one to six-year-olds. Further up the road is a modern school, there is also a youth centre where the school children can stay after school until the parents are off work. The school is free and we pay only about US$120 per child, per month for the day-care. Considering that the state gives us a tax-free annuity of US$1433 per annum, we just about break even on this! As of 2003 the tax-free child support allowance to Danish parents is as follows.

Child's age (years)	Annual Allowance; DKK/US$
0–2	12,900/1,633
3–6	11,700/1,481
7–17	9,200/1,165

This allowance is paid per child to all couples or single parents, regardless of income.

Our situation is not unusual, in most Danish residential neighbourhoods there will be childcare centres and schools within walking distance. These are good quality facilities with lots of toys and some open playgrounds around the building. The staff is a mixture of unskilled labour, often unemployed youth, put to work by the municipality, and skilled childcare specialists who undergo a three-year training course to qualify. The training is very comprehensive and the staff will be well versed in every practical and theoretical aspect of child upbringing, psychology and education. Danes in this business are dedicated people who really care about children and people in general and we have had nothing but good experiences in this regard.

If anything, lack of resources is the only problem. The price of childcare is heavily subsidised in Denmark, the fees parents pay only cover about one third of the actual cost, the rest is provided by public funding, therefore the demand tends to exceed supply and places in the different institutions are not always available. As both parents work in many Danish families, those who cannot find places for their offspring in public childcare centres must find other alternatives. Of course many people are more or less temporarily out of a job but they still regard themselves as part of the workforce and send their children away every day. If they cannot find a suitable childcare centre there are private freelancers and baby sitters available in most districts. In Denmark 60% of all one-year-olds and no less than 80% of all four-year-olds are cared for outside the home during business hours.

To cut costs there is sometimes a lack of staff at these centres, so the children fend for themselves a lot. In general, Danes don't mind that too much as it fits in well with a prevailing conviction that children should learn to become independent at an early age.

DOMESTIC HELP

Few Danish homes have maids and the idea of having a maid is not one that fits well with the egalitarian ideals of Danish society. Couples will of course use a babysitter on occasions and some upper middle-class families have a cleaning lady who comes in once or twice a week to do some of the chores. Expect to pay 30–40 kroner per hour for a teenage baby-sitter and 50–60 kroner per hour for a mature domestic helper. You can usually get this kind of assistance by asking around the neighbourhood if anybody is available.

It is possible to get live-in domestic help in Denmark. If you have room in your house some young girls (and boys) are available as au pair help. They usually stay for a year, getting some working experience before starting an education. Many work abroad in Europe or the United States but some prefer to stay near home with a Danish family. Some municipalities give support to families with small children needing domestic help through a scheme refunding part of the maid's salary, and it is worth checking out if this is available in your area. It is a typical Danish solution to the perennial problem of unrealistically high wages for inexperienced and unskilled workers – rather than reducing taxes and letting market forces control wages, taxes are increased and then refunded through complicated public support legislation.

As a foreigner you may not have your parents nearby to help you but in this respect you are not unique. In general, Danish couples do not expect help from their own parents. Older people in Denmark often stay in their careers until they are 67 (retirement age) or even older. It is mostly the low-skilled and low-paid workers who opt for the early retirement schemes available, people of influence and status stay on. Even when they retire, older people are often well-off and they do not have to depend on their children for support. They prefer to work in their garden, go to bingo sessions at the local community centre, they play snooker, collect stamps, watch television, take off to Spain for the winter if they can afford it – they are certainly not prepared to pitch in and help their children change nappies and prepare bottles for the third generation.

This attitude works both ways, however, and the working genera-tion seems to prefer it that way. Many middle-aged Danish people are not that close to their parents, they are not used to doing things together, except meeting for afternoon coffee every other Sunday or so and talking politely about how things are going. Few if any would like the old parents to live with them, so all parties really seem quite content with this configuration.

The Tough Children

The result of this family structure is that the children are on their own a lot. I think that we are here touching on one of the key aspects of Danish life, the root to many of the peculiarities in all levels of society that will surprise and sometimes shock newcomers.

One of the amazing things to me on arriving in Denmark from Asia was looking out over the playground near our house and seeing plenty of kids and no adults. The next day the situation was the same. In fact, as days and weeks went by, I never saw any grownups outside and I began to realise that this was the way it was in that country. The children are on their own. Sure, once in a while a mother would sit near the sandbox and keep an eye on her baby but once the baby became a toddler the mother would be inside like all the other mothers and fathers, cooking and cleaning, or outside working on the house or the garden – certainly not watching the child, nobody has time for just that.

Children are accustomed to this situation from an early age. Right after birth they are put in their separate cot, often Danish babies sleep in a room all of their own. Obviously there are diverse opinions regarding childcare in the country but many Danes believe that the baby should be toughened early on and left to cry if that is what it takes. People don't approach other people's children. In trains and on ferries toddlers move around but they do not interact with others, the other passengers act like they are not there. If you are used to picking up other people's babies and playing with them and coddling them, you have to be a little bit careful – some Danish parents will react to this unusual behaviour and may think that you are a bit strange.

In Denmark you will often see children playing unsupervised, although in this type of weather it is hardly surprising that no adult volunteers can be found!

There are liberal rules regarding maternity leave which at the moment is eight months for the mother (even the father is entitled to two weeks of paid leave after the delivery). Once this period is up the baby, which cannot even crawl at this stage, is often put in an institution all day, while the mother goes back to work. No matter how great the professionals are, that can only be a major upheaval for the baby and this is only the beginning. From now on the child lives in a world of its own, detached from the parents for much of the time. Together with the other children it must make its own rules.

Danish children often become contentious, they are not afraid of talking back to you and they become demanding and disputatious. The adults somehow don't mind this, they know it has to be like that if their kids are to survive.

Danes often kid with violence, strike each other playfully or make threats in a coy fashion. It can be a little unnerving if you are not used to it. Violence is a nationwide problem and notably taxi drivers, bus conductors, social workers and doctors are vulnerable. The amateur sociologist in me can't help wondering if the problem stems from the attitudes Danes learn as children.

YOUR SPOUSE IN DENMARK

If you don't have children you don't have to worry about all this of course. But you will worry about how your spouse gets along. If your wife/husband is not meeting people at work she/he might not be meeting any people at all. With no family nearby, spouses can become lonely and depressed. Many foreigners complain that the Danish society is an impossible one to penetrate and integrate into. I don't think that this is completely correct, but you will have to make a special effort.

Many foreigners do not want to integrate at all, they arrive as refugees to seek political liberties or economic support not available to them at home. Many of those foreigners understandably enough still prefer their own language and culture and food and customs and they tend to stick together in camps and public housing enclaves. When they or their children are encouraged to integrate they might even resent it.

However, if you are in Denmark out of choice there are things you can do to adjust and to help your spouse adjust. Danes prefer to stay in their own little house or apartment and they may not be prepared to mingle with their neighbours – some are but don't just take it for granted. Personally, I had a fairly shocking experience when we arrived and I started walking our kids to the play-school. To take a short-cut I sometimes walked along a bicycle track across a lawn, through a neighbouring estate. One day a man came up to me and my kids and said, "I thought you people had been told not to come through here." I was flabbergasted and did not know what he was on about, it had never occurred to me that the track could be anything but a public road. "This is a private road," the man said, "we cannot have strangers walking around here looking into our windows." Strangers! I mean we lived next to each other, our kids played together, the open track didn't come near any windows. Nevertheless, many Danes perceive their neighbours as a nuisance and a security threat, so if you or your spouse meet this attitude it will not make you feel particularly welcome. I walked the detour around the estate from then on so as not to upset anybody, even though I felt pretty silly doing it.

You may find that you and your family have the greatest neighbours in the world, I hope you do, but if you don't I also hope you can find some comfort in the fact that you will not be the first ones who discover that some Danes are difficult to get along with. Try to examine what you can do to make things work – not what all the other people should have done.

A good way to get along in Denmark is to exert yourself. Danes like active people who take the initiative and do things. Be prepared for some criticism when you stick your neck out, but in the long run it will pay off. First of all, learn the language, that in itself is an activity that will bring you out amongst people. Most local communities have

, community centres where you can engage yourself in ongoing activities. If you have a hobby become a member of that special society – you can be sure that there is such a society, no matter how obscure your interest is! When you go to meetings don't expect people to come and talk to you – you have to talk to them, they will be somewhat surprised but most likely pleasantly so, they will not be offended. Eventually you will find somebody you want to make friends with.

THE DANISH FAMILY

When you and your spouse start getting to know other couples you will find that the Danish family unit is much like families in other countries, except more emphasis is placed on the couple itself. In families with children, most are conventional, married couples. In about 16% of families the parents just live together and around 18% are families where the kids live with a single parent. Many married women keep their maiden name as surname. According to recent legislation gay couples are also allowed to register as married.

Married and de facto couples are treated somewhat differently in legislation with regards to taxation, inheritance and social benefits and since the Danish national pastime is to figure out how you can squeeze most money out of the state, much speculation is going on as to whether or not it is most beneficial to stay married or not. You will notice how each Danish magazine and paper has a column where readers can write in with questions, not about their love-life but something like, "I owe the kindergarten 5,000 kroner, my estranged husband hasn't paid his child-support for years, my mother wants to go to Spain for the winter, how do we best get the state to pay." A whole troupe of Danish lawyers make a career out of replying to those kinds of questions.

You will most likely find that among those couples who stay together quite traditional values are being upheld. Danes have experimented with feminism, just like most western and communist societies have, and some changes have indeed been made. Many Danish women now work or at least draw benefits as if they were available for work. But most are stuck in low-paid jobs, they seldom advance to decision making positions and they still end up doing most of the housework at home, even if they try to manage a career.

Sure, the Danish man will do the dishes and hang out the washing sometimes and in later years it has become fashionable for the 'new man' to become actively involved in his kids' upbringing. But equality between the sexes? Not really. The traditional roles and chores among the sexes are maintained in most families, the man fixes the car and the woman does the cooking, especially in the countryside. The Indian social researcher, G.P. Reddy (see list of books) made a note of this during his study and if you ever take a domestic morning flight from some provincial Danish town to the big city, it will be packed with businessmen and senior civil servants with their brief-cases, nearly all elderly, male Caucasians. Indications are that as long as it is the women in this world who give birth to the next generation, total equality of the sexes is a contradiction in terms.

IN SICKNESS AND IN HEALTH

If you have your family with you it is important to consider how they can be treated in case of sickness. You will be comforted to know that the Danish health service is good. It is not luxurious, you have to queue up for treatment on occasions, mistakes are made but on the whole you are in safe hands.

If you have obtained Danish residency status, health care is no problem, you just pass out your personal identity number and every-thing is available to you for free. That includes consultations with a doctor, specialist treatment and hospitalisation costs. This system doesn't give you unlimited choice, you will be appointed a physician somewhere near to your home. Nor does it include cosmetic treat-ment, physiotherapy and other non-vital care, you will have to pay for that yourself and dental care and prescription glasses are only partly subsidised.

Some Danes join Danmark A/S, a private health insurance company that will support some of that non-vital treatment. A fully comprehensive plan is available for foreigners and Danish expatriates who do not have any coverage at all. Even Danes have to be registered at a local municipality and pay local and national income tax to be eligible for free health care, citizenship in itself is not enough. As a non-resident you will naturally not be turned away from any Danish doctor if you are sick but you will be expected to settle the bill on the spot after treatment. Prices are quite reasonable, you pay about US$50 for an ordinary consultation and no more than US$15,000 for a cardiac bypass operation. Medicine in Denmark is, however, quite expensive as drugstores operate under a monopoly licence that impedes competition.

Danish Hospitals

During all the years I lived abroad I never spent the night in a hospital, except the time I stayed overnight with my wife after she gave birth to our twins. But in Denmark my luck ran out, I had a sporting injury playing badminton, had to be operated on and spent eight weeks with one foot in plaster. I was professionally and kindly treated all the way through and, apart from the nightmare of being disabled for months, it was a positive experience.

I had heard how overworked and unfriendly the staff were in Danish hospitals, how old the equipment, how poor the treatment. None of it turned out to be the case. I was well briefed about my condition and what was going to happen and the doctors and nurses all presented themselves politely to me and helped me in every way they could. When I went for checkups they sent me home in a taxi, something I would never waste money on myself.

So personally I appreciated the Danish health care system but I must admit that most Danish hospitals are old, some are very old and there is a constant lack of funds for upgrading and new equipment, as in many other countries where there is a national health service. There is only one class of service, everybody is handled the same way, wards are large and austere, you see people being treated in full view in the hallways, the food is adequate but no more than that. Salaries are low by international standards and therefore there is also a lack of staff. All emergencies are treated instantly but other operations you may have to wait months or sometimes years to have performed.

But of course the rich and well insured do not have to wait. There is always private health care available in Denmark and private hospitals will happily take you in, providing your credit rating checks out.

STARTING SCHOOL

If you have kids you will be concerned about their education and when it comes to education you have come to the right place. I know of no other place in the world where there is such a variety of high quality education available for everybody, young and old. Most of it is free or heavily subsidised. Just take your pick, from an evening class in embroidery at some laid-back school for the elderly, to a Ph.D. in economics at one of the most competitive business colleges there is. It is all there, actually the only problem you might have is choosing for your kids or yourself which subject to study, where and for how long but even this is taken care of at public student advisory centres. The Danes believe that education is the answer to all evils, including unemployment, juvenile delinquency and other social disorders and perhaps they are right.

Educating your child is compulsory. So although it is theoretically possible for you to teach your offspring the whole curriculum yourself, in practical terms you have to send your child to school. Most people send their children to a government school run by the local authority, a so-called *kommune skole*. There is one near every residential estate or village and it is totally free of charge, both tuition and textbooks. Some are large and others are small but educational standards vary very little from place to place.

About 11% of Danish kids attend private schools. If you choose a private school for your child you will have to pay a school fee, but

FOUNTAIN OF KNOWLEDGE

it will be small as most of the costs for private schools are covered by the government. To become approved for government support, private schools must meet some acceptable criteria regarding the educational standards, so basically the state curriculum is taught. Each private school, however, has its own different aim; it may be less authoritarian, or more so for that matter, than state schools or it may be associated with some educational, religious or philosophical movement. Private schools are mainly fairly small and located near the cities, but be prepared for you and your child to commute a bit further daily than if you select the local *kommune skole*.

Some private schools specialise in education for foreigners and special language groups. In the English language the Copenhagen International School (CIS) is the most prominent. It is frequented by expatriates and the diplomatic community but also by some Danish families who prefer a more stimulating environment for their kids. There are currently around 452 pupils in the school of no less than 51 different nationalities. The working language is English throughout but use of other languages is encouraged. Tuition fees vary according to the grades from 45,400 kroner per year for kindergarten to 84,000 kroner per year for high school. Additional fees apply for enrolment, extra tuition and bus service. More information including a colourful brochure and an application form is available from the school itself:

CIS
Hellerupvej 22-26
2900 Hellerup
Telephone: 3946 3300
Fax: 3161 2230
Website: http://www.cis-edu.dk

The Bernadotte School, also located in Hellerup north of Copenhagen is somewhat elitist and tuition is in Danish, although English is taught from the first grade.

Bernadotte Skolen
Hellerupvej 11
2900 Hellerup
Telephone: 3162 1215
Website: http://www.algonet.se/~bernadot/

Near the second largest town in Denmark, Århus, an international environment is available.

Interskolen
Engtoften
8260 Viby
Tel: 8611 4560
Fax: 8614 9670
Website: http://www.interskolen.com

In Denmark kids usually start schooling at six years of age in grade 0, as it is called. It is a kindergarten type of preschool class which is optional but a good start. The next year, when your child has turned or will turn seven, you will get a letter in the mail from the municipality, requesting that the child meet at the local school on some day in August for tuition – it is something like the army draft that comes later for the boys – the fun is over, you have to start getting up in the morning and the child has to begin the long haul on the road of learning.

Secondary Studies

For some kids the road comes to an end nine years later, that is the obligatory period of compulsory instruction. But most continue, some go on to complete a tenth year and 40% of the class will go on to high school which is another three years of secondary education. There are a number of options open for those who leave school in the ninth or tenth grade. There are many vocational trades to join and structured schemes to follow, which will eventually lead to a career as a licensed craftsman, many skilled workers do very well in Denmark and some go on to form their own small businesses.

For those who go on to high school there are two main streams, a mathematical stream and an arts/language stream. Within each, more subjects and priorities can be selected, this is equivalent to the A-levels in the British system. While the first nine years of schooling in Denmark are fairly relaxed with few examinations and tests, this is not the case for the secondary level. Here competition speeds up and the final secondary examination is of great importance for Danish students. Examinations start in May and last well into June with a number of written and oral tests. When students, who are all 18–19 years of age by now graduate, it is a huge relief for them and the whole family and celebrations last for days and weeks. The young graduates are simply called *nye studenter* in Danish (new students) and can easily be spotted on the streets, when they roam around singing, drinking beer, enjoying the early summer weather and displaying their little student caps in the national colours, white and red.

Advanced Education

Graduating from high school is an important turning point in most young kids' lives, especially so in Denmark because many teenagers also leave home at the end of that summer. Those that go on to university will often rent a small room near college, even if it is in their hometown and often with no roommate. Danish universities are not real campuses in the sense that things are going on there around the

Danish university students enjoying their time on campus. In Denmark many people remain students for quite a long time and a large percentage of Danes are well educated and highly qualified in their chosen fields. (Photo: Jens Henriksen)

clock. There are a few sporting and cultural activities available but come two o'clock and classrooms are locked, life comes to a standstill and most students stay in other places leading independent lives. Other youngsters go travelling at this stage or settle in some other town. Adult life is about to begin.

The actual high school examination results are of vital concern. Grades are given on a peculiar scale from 0 (worthless) to 13 (genius), 7–8 being average. To gain admission to the top institutions and later the top jobs you need a high score, way above average for university level medical, legal, economics and engineering faculties. Quotas for each tertiary institution and faculty in the country are calculated each year and the new entry requirements are announced each summer. All education is free, including tertiary level, so money is not an issue – only good grades will get you a place. Even then, Danish surveys show that doctors' daughters and lawyers' sons usually end up

131

studying medicine and law respectively, proving that genetic and social factors are of universal importance. In spite of Danish societies best efforts it seems that status is inherited in Denmark just like everywhere else.

Advanced studies are given a very high priority in Danish society but the choices facing the potential student are complicated to say the least. There are only three full-size universities in the country – in Copenhagen, Århus and Ålborg. But there are no less than 146 other educational institutions offering tertiary education in the fields of music, arts, film, theatre, library, journalism, business, engineering, architecture, education, social services, agriculture, pharmacy, physiotherapy and dentistry, to name some of them. In some careers, like banking, shipping, the oil-business and in the army you can get on the job training and gain professional qualifications while you work. There is student counselling available to guide the young high school graduate through this maze of possibilities. Even most Danes find it tough to select, gain access to and stay on and complete some tertiary education and foreigners must certainly expect some confusion in the beginning. Nevertheless, unless you posses some natural and quite exceptional business talent, tertiary education is the way to go if you want to make it in Denmark.

Denmark also has an incredible availability of adult education. I know of no surveys regarding this but it seems to me that in no other country will you find such a number of day-schools and night schools and all kinds of training courses on offer. Some are free and almost all are subsidised by the state. You can even get paid leave from your job to start a new course even if it is in no way related to your present job and the state will pick up the tab. Check out your local municipality for details.

The Danes are crazy about new learning, maybe the relative number of Danish homes with a personal computer is an indication – only the United States has more homes with a computer. The Danish system of libraries is another indication of their educational emphasis. All countries have libraries, but the Danish libraries are, in my opinion, the best. Each of the major branches is packed with all the latest newspapers, magazines and book titles, all computerised on an easy-access database. There are information leaflets on all matters you can think of, computers with free Internet access and if you cannot find what you need, the staff on duty will provide you with assistance.

DEFENDING THE COUNTRY

If you have a boy and he gains Danish citizenship he will receive a letter in the mail sometime during the year he turns 18. It will be from the armed forces and it will instruct him to be at the Draft Board at a certain date. If you have a girl she will be able to join the military voluntarily but she will not be drafted. If your son is found fit for service he will be drafted a year later. Many, however, have their service deferred a few years because of educational obligations. The young man does not necessarily have to become a soldier, if he would rather do some civil duties, all he has to do is say so and he can be

Young Danish men undertake military service but are offered a choice between military and civil duties.

attached to some charitable organisation or be sent abroad to do humanitarian work. The length of service varies but is usually nine months, less in the navy and up to two years if he is promoted to non-commissioned officer.

Even if he would like to become a solder, the young man may not be able to. Out of approximately 37,000 boys in one year only about 9,000 are needed as draftees, that is less than a quarter. There is simply not the political desire or money for a bigger army in Denmark. Apart from the draftees there are 4,000 officers and 13,000 other professionals in the military. About 70,000 people are organised in a kind of national guard called *hjemmeværnet* where they train for local defence in their spare time and keep a weapon at home. If all available reserves were mobilised the Danish fighting force would be 88,000.

The total lack of national antagonists and potential enemies is of course a problem for the top brass, who would like to see the military grow. During the Cold War much effort was put into portraying the countries in eastern Europe as strong and aggressive villains, we know now that this was something of a scam, without any foundation in the truth. Like all wars, the Cold War only served to obstruct European development and prosperity.

Today the military increasingly sees a new lifeline for itself as peacekeepers or peacemakers. But warriors and weapons manufacturers have, of course, always called themselves peacemakers. Denmark actively support international efforts of humanitarian intervention, a new concept where strong Western powers impose their values on weaker nations, even if it means destroying them, as witnessed in the former Yugoslavia and East Timor. Within NATO, Denmark participates in the Combined Joint Task Force (CJTF), a multinational rapid deployment force. Within the UN, Denmark plans to provide units for the Multinational UN Stand-BY Forces high Readiness Brigade. Currently (1999), 1,600 Danish military personnel serve abroad to defend Western interests in 12 different countries, mainly Kosovo (900) and Bosnia (600). More information is available from the Ministry of Defence website (http://www.fmn.dk).

Chapter Eight

LANGUAGE AND COMMUNICATION

COMMUNICATING WITH THE DANES

Luckily the Danes love to communicate, it is one of the paradoxes of Danish life, that although it may be hard to make the initial contact, once a Dane gets talking there is no stopping him. A foreigner once analogised talking to a Dane with shaking a ketchup bottle – first nothing comes out and then suddenly everything at once.

In spite of the small size of the country there are great regional differences in the way people communicate, especially with strangers. Traditionally, people in the rural districts of western and northern Jutland are calm and careful in choosing their words and their dialect is quite unlike the official Danish. Expect contacts to take a little longer to establish if you end up in that part of the countryside.

The city-slickers in and around Copenhagen are different. They are typically fast-talking, more open and sometimes shockingly frank in their expressions. If an urban Dane does not like the way your hair or your dress looks or the way you do things he will come right out and tell you so. He will also expect you to speak up if you do not agree with him. Nobody is offended by a quick argument, feelings are left unhurt and everybody goes on with their business afterwards, the matter is soon forgotten. Nobody has 'lost face,' that is just the way communication is conducted.

Body language is very subtle, in fact Danes regularly poke fun at 'southerners' (meaning southern Europeans like Italians, Frenchmen and Spaniards) for their rich bodily expressions, including delicate hand movements and waving arms. That sort of thing is regarded as quite ridiculous in Denmark but on the other hand I do not recall Danes ever having been unintentionally offended by certain gestures, they simply do not pay too much attention to them. Anyway, it takes quite a lot to offend a Dane, although a shaken fist or the universal 'finger' of course will do it. Apart from that the Danes prefer to let their mouths do the talking.

DIFFERENT LANGUAGES

Being a small nation and a quite open-minded culture, the Danes have had to accept other languages. In general they have even made a deed out of necessity and most Danes speak two or more languages. Most younger Danes (below the age of say 40 or even 50) will be able to communicate with you in fairly fluent English. English is taught in all schools from grade four and upwards and even before that most kids will pick up some. English has become the language of international trade and business and since Denmark does a lot of trade the language is compulsory curriculum. Once you get to high school and certainly university level education, many textbooks will simply not be available in translations, so students must be fluent in English to complete their education.

There may be members of the senior generation who have either not taken all that much English in the older educational system or who have forgotten it for lack of regular usage but these people are fast becoming a minority. Apart from business, English is also today the language of international entertainment and news and the Danish kids watch MTV and CNN and switch on the Internet just like kids all over the world. What didn't work out for Esperanto – to become a universal world language – English is now quickly about to accomplish.

The other contestants in the race for global linguistic supremacy like French and Spanish are these days left trailing behind. However, within the European Union, French is still used quite a lot and Danes who fancy a lucrative career as an EU bureaucrat will select French at high school level. Some German is also compulsory during school to keep relations with that big neighbour to the south cordial and many more can be optionally selected, although none of these languages have had the impact on modern Danish communication that English has. In fact, the Danish language is still evolving and more and more English words and expressions are being incorporated into it.

The electronic media is very much a part of all this and American and English shows and movies are not dubbed like they are in other major languages, they are shown with the original soundtrack and subtitles. So when you go to the movies or watch television you can learn a fair bit of Danish by just checking the subtitles, picking out the words and translating for yourself.

The Scandinavian Brotherhood

The Scandinavian languages are a special case. Danish is a language within the Germanic group of languages, with special affinities to the Latin based languages of southern Europe and the German and Nordic vocabulary and grammar of the north. Within the group of five Nordic countries (Denmark, Norway, Sweden, Iceland and Finland) three (Denmark, Norway and Sweden) constitute a tightly knit fraternity – the Scandinavian countries. While the languages of Iceland and

137

Finland are totally different to Danish, Norwegian and Swedish are somewhat similar.

Modern Norwegian in particular is close to Danish, when you see it written it is hard to tell the difference, although the pronunciation makes it a bit harder to pick up (Norway has in recent years introduced a second official language based on an older version which differs more from Danish).

Swedish is different but still quite similar to Danish and, especially in the Eastern part of Denmark, where people on each side of the Øresund Strait watch each other's television shows, communication is no problem. Some Danes, however, find Swedish awkward to understand and prefer to switch to English when they meet up with members of their 'brotherhood people' (this term is actually used in official jargon).

DANISH NAMES

Even if you have no ambitions of becoming an expert in the finer details of Scandinavian verbiage, I would advise you to just look a bit into Danish names. When you meet Danes you will be presented with new names all the time and when you travel in the country some understanding of locality names will help you get around.

Consider the fact that about two thirds of all Danes have a surname ending with 'sen.' Up until just a few generations ago most Danes did not have family names at all, only educated, upper-class clans and the aristocracy carried the family name through generations. In the country common folk were just named after their father so that Peter's son was called Søren Petersen ('sen' being a variation of the word 'son'), his son Hans Sørensen and so on. In 1856 a law was passed that all citizens should be identified by a minimum of two names, one being a family surname, so most people ended up carrying a 'sen' name forward.

Today on the list of most common Danish surnames no less than the 21 top names end with a 'sen' and out of the top 50 names only five are not 'sen' names. The top five are: Jensen, Nielsen, Hansen, Pedersen and Andersen – and it just goes on and on from there. Since the most common boys' names are also Jens, Hans, Peter, Niels, Jørgen and Lars (in that order) and countless people are called Jens Jensen and Niels Nielsen and so on, it is no wonder that newcomers find Danish names confusing, especially boys names as they are frequently being reused and repeated in the surnames.

If you are one of those who find it difficult to remember Danish names maybe you can take some comfort in the following true story.

Where we stay in Denmark there are 15 houses in the estate, our house is number 12. Next door in 11 lives a little boy called Anders, the problem is that in house 6 there is also an Anders, an adult, his son is Rasmus. Anders in 11 has a brother, he is also called Rasmus while Anders in 6 has another son called Jakob. In house 15 also lives a Jacob, who has a son called Peter. House 13 recently changed hands, the new owner is Peder, pronounced like Peter, he has a son named Thomas – so did the previous owner whose name was Erik – just like the man in number 10.

Confused? Well, there is more; Peder has another son, Niels. In house 2 also lives a Niels, his brother is called Peter, much like the other Niels's father. Next to Peter, in house 1, lives a man named Henrik – only in the other house next door at number 3 the man is also called Henrik, his son is Jacob, Jens Jacob actually but there is another Jens – in house 5, Jens Erik is his name. Jens Erik has a son called Daniel – so do we, our Daniel is the same age incidentally. And I am not the only Morten, the boy in house 14 is also Morten. Morten's father's name is Hans, but the man in number 8 is also Hans, Hans Henrik actually. Hans Henriks's neighbour is called Thomas – no, this is not the Thomas in 13, the older Thomas lives in number 9. Hans Henrik has another son, Mads, but Mads is also the name of the boy in house 4 – his father is called Ole. Ole has another son, called Anders, different from the two Anders in 6 and 11. Come to think of it my brother-in-law who lives nearby is also called Ole, he has a son called Mathias. The Mads in house 8 who is not Ole's son has another brother apart from Rasmus – he is also called Mathias. Did you get that? It certainly took a while before I did!

NAMES OF PLACES

When you drive around the place you may be confused with the locality names. I read one travel story in a British magazine by a couple who had toured Denmark. In general they were very enthusiastic about the whole trip. One of their only adverse comments was, "We had a hard time distinguishing the names of different places and towns."

Denmark is an ancient culture, every little nook and cranny has been occupied for centuries and they all have names – often old names that have long ago lost their original significance. If you look at how most of the names are composed out of old words often referring to features in the terrain you may be able to better tell them apart and memorise them. I must add that I find this pretty difficult myself but breaking down the composite names a little surely helps.

Danish Word	Meaning	Example
Mark	Field	Danmark, Søndermarken
Havn	Harbour	København,
By	Town	Rødby, Lyngby
Borg	Castle	Kalundborg, Silkeborg
Ø	Island	Samsø, Rømø
Å	River	Århus, Grenå
Hus	House	Husby, Blokhus
Bæk	Creek	Vedbæk, Holbæk
Holm	Island	Bornholm, Hørsholm
Bro	Bridge	Hobro, Bjerringbro
Skov	Forest	Nakskov, Vodskov
Lund	Park	Albertslund,

Bjerg	Mountain	Esbjerg, Gilbjerg Hoved
Hoved	Head	Knudshoved,
Gård	Farm	Hovedgård, Alsgårde
Høj	Hill	Brønshøj, Ishøj
Rød	Clearing	Hillerød, Birkerød
Sted	Place	Ringsted, Vigersted
Sund	Strait	Frederikssund,
Strand	Beach	Greve Strand, Strandby

The following terms are ones you are likely to find when reading a map:

Vej	Road
Gade	Street
Stræde	Narrow street
Torv	Market place
Plads	Square

PICKING UP DANISH

Some visitors to Denmark see it as a courtesy to learn to say *tak* instead of thank you, *god dag* instead of hello and that sort of thing but really it is not absolutely necessary – those will be the words anybody knows in English anyway and the Danes will just find the whole thing slightly odd. You are better off sticking to English all the way through, especially if it is your first language or you speak it equally well.

If you have a special hobby of learning new languages (some people actually enjoy that!) or if you plan to stay and work and integrate into society you should read on from here and then go on to study from a proper textbook as listed in the back of this book or enrol in a language course. There are plenty of day and evening courses available teaching Danish for foreigners. The authorities have some problems getting part of the foreign community to integrate, especially aliens on refugee status, so Danish language tuition is generally encouraged.

If that is what you want to do, integrate, you may find it a disadvantage that English is so widely understood and spoken in Denmark. Most people you meet would probably prefer to switch to English to practise their own skills, rather than listen to you struggling to find the words in their own language. Be firm and insist on staying with Danish – it is the only way you will ever be any good at it.

And after all, fluency in the local language is a prerequisite for total integration into any society. You will never really be part of the group if the Danes around you have to switch to another language every time you have to be part of the conversation. Foreigners who learn the language are quickly accepted in Denmark and have an easier time finding friends and a job. Adopted children and others who learn the language fluently are not discriminated against. Others who insist on sticking to their own language and culture may be in for a harder time, those are the realities that you have to face whether you like it or not. Skin colour, race and religion do not matter, the language is the key if you want to be 'one of them' in Denmark.

As you start to use the language you will notice that using a new language is not just a matter of memorising technical grammar and translating word by word. The Danes simply discuss matters differently and the equivalent words are used more or less frequently and with slightly different connotations than in English. Take a word like love. Sure, in Danish there is a similar term, *kærlighed* for the noun and *at elske* for the verb. "I love you" is said *jeg elsker dig* but in Danish those words are mostly used to refer to a man/woman attraction, with a physical innuendo. It is not normal for parents to say, "I love you/*jeg elsker dig,*" to their child at bedtime as would be natural for an American. In this way, Danes are not as affectionate.

You cannot learn to speak Danish in a few pages and I am no language tutor but I would like to provide you with a subjective introduction to some aspects of the grammar and vocabulary of the language, based on my own experiences and my work with foreigners visiting Denmark. So the rest of the chapter is a take-it-or-leave-it option for those who might be contemplating picking up the lingo.

The Alphabet and Pronunciations

As you might have observed form the words and names listed previously there are three extra letters in Danish, they are placed at the end of the alphabet. They are:

Æ/æ = ae
Ø/ø = oe
Å/å = aa

They are used frequently, "W" is however used less in Danish. As you might notice when you hear it, Danish is spoken quite monotonously, without great variations in tone and strength and it is spoken a lot more slowly than Spanish for instance and other Latin based languages. However, often the letters and words are blurred together and that can sometimes make it harder to understand.

Some letters are not pronounced at all like "ve" in *have* (to have/ to get) or "ge" in *tage* (to take). Note how many letters are missing in the spoken version. For example:

- *Vil du have en kop kaffe?*
"Would you like a cup of coffee?" becomes;
Ve' du ha' en kop kaff? when spoken, or;

- *Tager du med til stranden?*
"Are you coming along to the beach?" becomes;
Ta'r du me' ti' stran'en?

"R" is not rolled but is flat, pronounced from the back of the mouth without flapping the tongue. However, "D" is special. Instead of a proper "D" like in D-Day, the Danes use a full, soft sound that sort of stays in the mouth, a so-called "soft D." If you do take a language course I doubt if you will manage to complete it without having to pass the test of saying: *Rødgrød med fløde* (Red pudding with cream – a jelly-like desert) Using the special Danish "D" – few pass this test, even the other Scandinavians cannot do it and the Danes bend over with laughter when they try.

When you see a Danish text it will be easier for you to pick the language to pieces, as many words are spelled similarly to English, especially the Latin based ones and you will not be distracted by the strange pronunciations. You will notice how capital letters are used a lot less in Danish, only names – not adjectives and adverbs - are in capital letters. For example: *I England taler man engelsk* (In England you speak English).

A Bit of Grammar – Nouns and Verbs

There are many little bits and pieces where the grammar of Danish and English differ. Let me mention a few that come to mind:

In Danish there are two genders of nouns, as there are in many other European languages but it can be a bit confusing.

- *Et hus, huset, det hus, et andet hus.* (A house, the house, that house, another house.) but;
- *En stol, stolen, den stol, en anden stol.* (A chair, the chair, that chair, another chair.)

So that makes Danish a bit complicated since you have to learn the gender of each noun. (Note that the ending "en" substitutes for the English "the" in front of the noun.)

The gender is also important for saying:

• *Han kan lide sit hus. Hun kan lide sin stol.* (He likes his house. She likes her chair.)

However, the verbs are easier as there is no I am, you are, he/she/ it is etc. The verbs are all one form, so:

• *Jeg løber, han løber, vi løber.* (I run, he runs, we run.)

There are many differences in how verbs are used to express present and future activities but in general Danish is simpler and less varied than English. For instance:

• *Jeg spiller bold.* (I play ball.)

• *Jeg hedder Niels.* (I am Niels.)

• *Jeg er fra England.* (I come from England.)

All verbs end in "er" in present tense, furthermore, the present tense is often used for the future, like:

• *Jeg rejser i morgen.* (I will travel tomorrow.)

Past tense is signified with a "te" or a "de" ending, like:

• *Jeg rejste i går.* (I travelled yesterday.) Or;

• *Han vågnede hurtigt.* (He woke up quickly.)

But, as in English, there are a number of irregular verbs to memorise. This is a fairly time consuming process.

The present perfect is a "t" or an "et" ending, like:

• *Jeg har rejst meget.* (I have travelled a lot.)

In general there are fewer words for saying the same thing. But then English is known for containing a particularly great many words, which the user can select depending on how sophisticatedly he is able to manipulate the language!

Adjectives and Adverbs

In English adverbs are adjectives with a "ly" ending. In Danish the letter "t" is used in the transformation. For example:

- *En hurtig handel, det blev hurtigt gjort.* (A quick deal, that was quickly done.)

  If the noun is plural an "e" is added to the adjective, like:
- *To hurtige handler.* (Two quick deals.)

  The adjective also changes with gender, so it is:
- *Et nyt hus, en ny stol.* (A new house, a new chair)

  Meanwhile, adverbs remain unchanged regardless of gender and number of the noun.

  As in English, adjectives come in three forms – positive, comparative and superlative, like:
- *Langsom, langsommere, langsomst.* (Slow, slower, slowest.)

  And likewise, there are a number of exceptions:
- *Mange, flere, flest.* (Many, more, most.)

  Adverbs can also be irregular:
- *Jeg vil gerne, jeg vil hellere, jeg vil helst.* (I would like, I would rather, I would preferably.)

  Maybe your teacher can explain to you the deeper significance of all this. There are people who study the finer details of languages – and the rest of us who just speak them!

VOCABULARY

The following few pages list some words which will be helpful in getting you started with the language and allow you to recognise some key words in Danish. Try learning a few a day and look for them on signs or while watching television. Good luck.

Danish	English		
Aften	Evening	Bage	Bake
Aldrig	Never	Bagefter	Afterwards
Anden	Another	Begynde	Begin
April	April	Behøve	Need
August	August	Benzin	Petrol
Bad	Bath	Besøge	Visit
		Betale	Pay

Bibliotek	Library	Dreje	Turn
Bil	Car	Dreng	Boy
Billed	Picture	Drikke	Drink
Billig	Cheap	Dronning	Queen
Biograf	Cinema	Du	You
Blomst	Flower	Dum	Stupid
Blyant	Pencil	Dygtig	Skilful
Blæse	Blow	Død	Dead
Bord	Table	Dårlig	Bad
Brev	Letter	Efter	After
Briller	Glasses	Efterår	Fall
Bror	Brother	Egen	Own
Bruge	Use	Elev	Pupil
Brun	Brown	Elske	Love
Brød	Bread	End	Than
Bukser	Pants	Far	Father
Butik	Shop	Farfar	Grandfather (paternal)
Bygning	Building		
Bøje	Bend	Farvel	Goodbye
Båd	Boat	Ferie	Holiday
Cykel	Bicycle	Fest	Party
Cykle	Ride a bicycle	Fjernsyn	Television
Dag	Day	Flaske	Bottle
Dame	Lady	Flere	More
Dansk	Danish	Flot	Handsome
Dansker	Dane	Foldbold	Football
Datter	Daughter	Folk	People
Dav	Hello	Fordi	Because
Dejlig	Nice	Forelske	Fall in love
Der	There	Forkert	Wrong
Derhen	Over there	Forklare	Explain
Derop	Up there	Forretning	Business
Det	It	Forstå	Understand

147

Fortsætte	Continue	Hej	Hi
Fortælle	Tell	Hun	She
Forår	Spring	Huske	Remember
Fra	From	Hvad	What
Fredag	Friday	Hvem	Who
Fremmed	Strange	Hvid	White
Frokost	Lunch	Hvor	Where
Fryse	Freeze	Hvordan	How
Fuld	Full	Hvorfor	Why
Fylde	Fill	Hvornår	When
Færdig	Finished	Høre	Hear
Færge	Ferry	Hånd	Hand
Før	Before	I	In
Gaffel	Fork	Ikke	Not
Gammel	Old	Ind	Inside
Gang	Hall	Indgang	Entrance
Gave	Present	Ingen	None
Gennem	Through	Invitere	Invite
Gentage	Repeat	Ja	Yes
God	Good	Jeg	I
Goddag	Hello	Jo	Yes
Grad	Degree	Jul	Christmas
Græde	Cry	Kage	Cake
Grøn	Green	Kartoffel	Potato
Grå	Grey	Kende	Know
Gul	Yellow	Kjole	Dress
Guld	Gold	Klokken	Time
Gæst	Visitor	Kniv	Knife
Gå	Walk	Kold	Cold
Halv	Half	Komme	Come
Han	He	Kone	Wife
Handle	Deal	Kop	Cup
Herre	Gentleman	Koste	Cost

Krop	Body	Ny	New
Købe	Buy	Når	When
Kød	Meat	Og	And
Køre	Drive	Op	Up
Langsom	Slow	Ord	Word
Leje	Rent	Over	Over
Lidt	A little	Oversætte	Translate
Lille	Small	Penge	Money
Lukket	Closed	Pige	Girl
Lytte	Listen	Plade	Plate or record
Læge	Doctor	Politi	Police
Lære	Learn or teach	Posthus	Post office
Lærer	Teacher	Pris	Price
Læse	Read	På	On
Lørdag	Saturday	Påske	Easter
Mad	Food	Rejse	Travel
Mand	Man	Ren	Clean
Mandag	Monday	Rigtig	Correct
Middag	Dinner	Ringe	Call
Mig	Me	Se	Look
Minut	Minute	Sejle	Sail
Mor	Mother	Seng	Bed
Morfar	Grandfather (maternal)	Sen	Late
		Sende	Send
Morgen	Morning	Sko	Shoes
Mælk	Milk	Skole	School
Nabo	Neighbor	Sky	Cloud
Nat	Night	Smage	Taste
Ned	Down	Smuk	Beautiful
Nej	No	Snakke	Talk
Nogle	Some	Sne	Snow
Nord	North	Sol	Sun
Nu	Now	Sommer	Summer

149

Sort	Black	Vejr	Weather
Sove	Sleep	Ven	Friend
Spille	Play	Veninde	Girlfriend
Sprog	Language	Venlig	Friendly
Stor	Big	Vente	Wait
Syd	South	Verden	World
Søn	Son	Vest	West
Søndag	Sunday	Vi	We
Tage	Take	Vin	Wine
Tak	Thank you	Vinter	Winter
Tale	Speak	Vække	Wake up
Tand	Tooth	Værelse	Room
Tandlæge	Dentist	Vågne	Wake or awake
Taske	Bag	Øje	Eye
Tid	Time	Øl	Beer
Time	Hour	Øre	Ear or cents
Ting	Thing or item	Øst	East
Tirsdag	Tuesday	Åben	Open
Tit	Often	År	Year
Tog	Train		
Told	Customs		
Torsdag	Thursday		
Tøj	Clothes		
Tørstig	Thirsty		
Ud	Out		
Uden	Without		
Udgang	Exit		
Udlænding	Foreigner		
Uge	Week		
Undskyld	I am sorry		
Vand	Water		
Varm	Warm		
Vaske	Wash		

— *Chapter Nine* —

SOCIALISING WITH THE DANES

Once you have arrived in Denmark, settled in and learnt how to communicate with people, you will want to start getting to know the locals and go out socialising with them. Well, this is one thing the Danes love to do but there are some peculiarities here that you should be aware of.

EVENTS CAREFULLY ORGANISED

First of all, the key word in Danish society is structure. If a person turns 30 or 40 or 50 there is no way he will celebrate it by letting the word out that everybody can come over maybe sometime during the day for a snack and a beer. For goodness sake, do not drop in on him unexpectedly on his birthday to wish him good luck, anticipating some kind of open house situation. If you turned up at his home uninvited it would be terribly embarrassing for him and his guests, the Danes simply do not know how to tackle such informal and improvised situations.

What the Danes call 'round' birthdays are planned months, sometimes years, in advance and might turn out to be the highlight of a person's life-cycle. When my mother turned 50 she invited everybody she knew and everybody who had ever meant anything to her during her youth to a seaside resort hotel and wined and dined them all afternoon, all night and the next morning as well. I lived abroad in the UK at the time and had just got married and I drove across to meet all these people whom I hardly remembered and have not seen since. When my mother turned 70, she threw a similar party. They constituted the peak of her social life.

Recently my wife and I have been invited to a few other 'round' birthdays. My uncle turned 60, my mother-in-law as well, our neighbour turned 40 and invited everybody (some other neighbour also turned 40 but only assembled family – much to the annoyance of those casual friends who did not get invited!). If you know Danes well it is very likely that you will find yourself invited to an occasion like this. In my experience these parties seem to follow a uniform standard configuration. Here is roughly what you can expect.

You are Invited to a Party

You will get an invitation in the mail, usually a month before the event, perhaps longer. The invitation will include you and your spouse, but no children please. You are expected to reply and, once you have signed on, only death or something equivalent is a valid excuse for not attending.

When you go, bring a gift. Money is a no-no. If you give Danes money you are implying that they are unable to finance their own lives. The gift must be something personal. Sometimes the occasion will be a joint celebration, like a wedding anniversary or a couple lumping two birthdays into one, so it is more appropriate to give something they will need between them, like an item for their home. It is quite acceptable to call up and ask what they would like to get. If you don't know what to buy, pitch in with somebody who knows the person better and share a gift – this way you end up just giving money after all. Danish gifts are not lavish, 150–200 kroner worth per guest or couple is considered appropriate, more only if you are close family. As an extra you can always bring flowers when you arrive, and a bottle of wine is always appreciated on practically any occasion.

Dress is formal, but this is one area where you should have no problems as Danes are not known as particularly good dressers. An ordinary business suit is considered adequate for the men and any ready-to-wear dress is fine for the ladies. Only at high society gatherings are tuxedos in fashion with fancy designer evening gowns for the ladies – and in that case a black-tie warning will be specified on the invitation. I have noticed that many people turn up for formal parties in what could be termed neat casual wear, or jeans with a shirt and tie, so don't worry too much about all this.

A Danish Dinner Celebration

In this case you are usually invited to attend late in the afternoon. The venue will often be the local community hall, clubhouse or hotel, since 30 or 40 or more people will attend and few homes are big enough for this. There will be little Danish paper flags at the nearest road-junction to guide you on your way and more flags at the entrance to the dining hall. At birthdays and international soccer games the Danes really display the national colours of white and red, the so-called *Dannebrog* flag.

Be on time, everybody else will be. After a welcome drink all guests are seated at a large table. This is it, this is where you will be for the rest of the night. You cannot just grab a seat somewhere, the table-plan has been designed carefully by your hosts in advance and there will be little name cards at each seat. Couples are split up, if you arrived with a partner, it is just too bad, you are on your own now. If you are a man, you are supposed to pay special attention to the lady on your right. Help her get seated and try to think of something bright to say, although you probably don't know her very well.

The menu will most likely be a three-course dinner with a starter, main course and dessert. The starter used to be a soup in the old days but is more likely now to be a seafood dish, like smoked salmon, crab-meat or prawns, with a bit of salad and bread. White wine is served with this. At this stage the host will propose a toast and bid everybody welcome, and afterwards you will be able to get in on the conversation going on around you.

Getting into the Conversation

Of course the others at the table may know one another a lot better than you do. Try not to get into the stereotype contribution to the conversation of, "So, how do you do things in (whichever country you come from) ?" Your new friends only ask this question out of politeness, in actual fact, they probably couldn't care less about conditions in your home country and they are only waiting for a chance to get back to the subjects that really interest them. You would do better to tune into those and speak your mind.

The Dinner Goes On and On and On ...

After a while the main course is served. Don't get up from the table unless you have to. Your host probably has a catering service or some neighbours to help out with all the cooking and serving. The meal is some kind of steak, pork, beef or veal with boiled or baked potatoes, gravy and some other vegetables and greens.

Red wine is served with the main course but there is no real obligation to drink, cold water will be provided as well. If you don't want a lot to drink just sip at your glass and leave it full – if you do need something to help you get through the night, empty it at every toast and the waiter or the people around you will make sure it is filled up.

Towards the end of the main course the dinner turns into a kind of 'This is Your Life' event. Different people close to the celebrated person or couple will get up and make a speech prepared for the occasion. There will be songs as well, usually written by family members, putting new words to a well known Danish tune. If you cannot write yourself there are agencies in Denmark who advertise in the newspapers offering song-writing services. You just provide the agent with details of the person in question and for a fee you will be provided with a suitable text. After each session the speaker will propose a toast and everybody gets up and utters the famous *"skål"* with a raised glass.

Some speeches and songs are supposed to be funny. Something like, "Do you remember the time you fell down from the barn roof, and the time your car wouldn't start when you had to bring your wife to the delivery room?" – that sort of thing is usually funny in retrospect. You may not understand it all but the Danes will, and they will all be literally screaming with laughter, you have to see this to believe it.

Then the next speaker will change the tune, maybe it is the father talking about his little girl when he walked her to school for the first time and how she cheered him up when he was ill. Don't be surprised if the 'little girl,' who now happens to be a 40-year-old, tougher-than-nails matron, starts sobbing with emotion, it is all very touching.

The Party is Over

The dessert is usually ice-cream or cake or both and while Danish meats and flavourings are nothing special, the desserts often are. Danish cakes and pastries are some of the best in the world. Coffee is served, as well as sherry, port or brandy with the desert. Finally the party is disintegrating a bit and you can feel free to stretch your legs while walking around and talking to people you know better. The tone

becomes more informal, since the initial collective nervousness is wearing off and the liquor is having its effect. Maybe you can even start to enjoy yourself a bit.

You can smoke at any time during the meal, although most do so in little breaks between courses. Many Danes smoke and they are light-years behind places like the United States in smoking regulation and people will light up in restaurants and at the office without asking for consent. Smoking is regarded as some kind of human right – and human rights are sacred stuff.

You can feel free to leave at this point. Working couples with young children who have to get up in the morning usually do. The very young and the elderly will stay, the big dinner table is cleared and there will be dancing until the early hours of the morning, when maybe a snack of sandwiches with sausages and pates are served before the party is finally over.

OCCASIONS TO CELEBRATE

So this is the how most Danes will celebrate a big occasion. With their tribal traditions and loose family ties, Danes function best in little groups, where they all know each other well. That is why they prefer structured formats for larger events. Even abroad in expatriate communities, Danes will party like this amongst themselves, shunning the internationally accepted arrangements of buffet dinners and come-as-you-are barbecues. Obviously young kids and teenagers get together informally during weekends and improvise a party but most official celebrations will have this very structured and predictable layout.

You are most likely to be invited to attend birthdays, weddings and anniversaries, when the Danes are prepared to invite a larger crowd. Other family events are usually that – events within the family. The big family occasions in Denmark are the christening of a newborn, confirmation of the baptism when the child is about 14 years of age, weddings and funerals. I have personally never attended any such occasion in Denmark, except my grandfather's funeral ten years ago, so that goes to show that for these events only the very inner family circle is invited.

The christening of a newborn is a religious event where the closest family members gather at the local church. The priest will name and bless the child near the altar and the guests will be treated to a dinner afterwards.

The confirmation is an important occasion for most teenagers. This is also strictly a Christian tradition where the young people in church confirm their belief in the principles of Christianity. After the church ceremony there will be a party and a dinner where the older generation accepts the young person as an adult in formal and not so formal speeches. The kid is honoured and praised for a day and endowed with new clothes and expensive gifts like a fancy new bicycle, a stereo, camping equipment and that sort of thing.

The wedding can either be a full-blown Christian church wedding with the bride dressed all in white, or it can be a more solemn arrangement at the City Hall for those who do not pay as much attention to religious affairs. The wedding is usually paid for by the bride's parents – the first one that is, after that Daddy's little girl is on her own and if she divorces and remarries later it will be at her own expense! Some couples will make a big thing out of their wedding and invite everybody they know for a traditional dinner party. Others will keep it within the family and then there are some who will keep it out of the family altogether and just have a couple of close friends to tag along as witnesses. It is all a matter of temperament and taste.

The funeral is obviously not a celebration and there is no dinner involved. Often the funeral will be announced publicly in advance so that everybody concerned can send flowers or attend. Ask a flower shop which selection is appropriate if you attend or send a wreath. If somebody you are at all associated with dies it is good courtesy to show up and pay your last respects. You do not have to stay for coffee and cakes afterwards, just attend the church and the grave-site as the coffin is buried. A close relative as well as a pastor will speak. Wear black or subdued clothing and keep at the back and let the closest family members run the show, just expressing your condolences by being there will be sufficient.

DANES AND RELIGION

Ordinarily the Danes are not really a religious people, the Church is integrated with the state and it is just a fact of life that few Danes really pay very much attention to. Around 92% of the population are members of the state sponsored Protestant Church and all newborns join automatically. The rest have either left to become members of another faith or are either atheists or agnostic. Only three percent of Danes, mostly older people, attend church twice a month or more, according to a 1987 survey and the number is dropping. However, in other surveys most Danes consistently claim that they believe in God, especially elderly women. About 50% of Danes attend church a few times a year, most for the Christmas and Easter services.

Most religious dates are occasions that have lost any real spiritual meaning to the Danish population. A look at the Danish social calendar will show a mixture of civil and religious dates that to the Danes mean only one thing – time off! Time off to do what the Danes love the most: work at home, travel, socialise and party.

THE DANISH SOCIAL YEAR

The following dates are the most significant holidays or celebrations on the Danish calendar.

New Year's Day, January 1: A holiday celebrating the start of the calendar year.

Shrovetide, late February: Originally the evening before a religious fasting period. Today a fancy dress carnival for kids, the kids will dress up and knock on doors for handouts. They will also gather to beat on a wooden barrel with little baseball bats. When the barrel breaks, candy and fruits drop out and the lucky kid is named King (or Queen) of *Fastelavn*.

Danish children enjoying the traditional Shrovetide celebrations.

159

Easter, end of March/beginning April: The resurrection of Christ. Today an excuse for taking a week off to go skiing in Norway or the Alps or to stay at home and dig up the garden.

April Fool's Day, April 1: The Danes love this kind of slapstick stuff. If the radio announces rationing of petrol or war with Sweden on this date don't be alarmed, it is just a joke!

May Day, May 1: The old socialist workers' day and the old-timers in the trade unions still gather around Danish parks. With the 'New World Order' this day has lost much of its significance and it is not even a holiday!

Store Bededag, May, (fourth Friday after Easter): Meaning "The Great Prayer's Day," it is a peculiar religious date unique to Denmark that lumps together different religious dates into one occasion. Basically just another day off during a nice time of year.

Ascension Day, end of May: Holiday 40 days after Easter commemorating the ascension of Christ.

Whitsuntide, beginning of June: Another nice spring holiday, celebrates the return of the Holy Spirit to earth.

Grundlovsdag, June 5: Meaning "Constitutional Day," a kind of national day, here they memorialise the first Danish constitution in 1849, an opportunity for the politicians to speak their minds on the state of the nation while the voters bask in the sunshine drinking beer.

Midsummer Evening, June 23: This is not a holiday but Danes gather all over the country to celebrate the next day, the longest and brightest of the year. A bonfire is lit, sometimes including a dummy witch, representing the evil spirits of darkness. You sing songs, roast hot-dogs on the embers afterwards and drink wine – quite a pleasant event, don't miss it!

Advent, December: As a warm-up, every Sunday before Christmas most Danes celebrate with candles and decorations.

In celebration of the longest day of the year bonfires are lit on Midsummer Evening. In a climate such as Denmark's the day of most sunshine is indeed cause for celebration.

Christmas Evening, December 24: The big day for all Danish kids and some adults as well. This is when Danes get together with their closest family and eat and sing and dance around the Christmas tree and exchange presents. The next two days are holidays and Danes often go visiting more distant family and friends for Christmas lunches, where they eat loads of open-faced sandwiches and drink, the police force is busy staking out the main traffic arteries on the lookout for drunken drivers.

New Year's Eve, December 31: The worldwide party-night, Denmark is no exception, it is not a holiday but the next day simply has to be!

So, although many of the national holidays have religious affiliations, it is really only Christmas that has retained its Christian substance in any significant way among the Danes. As a whole the

161

Danes are not a spiritual people, their thinking is mainly materialistic and scientific by nature. That does not mean that you will not find all kinds of supernatural groupings and sects around the periphery of society, experimenting with alternative lifestyles but you have to look very hard and these minorities are basically without influence.

If anything spiritual has been left over in Danish society it is little superstitious reflexes like not walking underneath a ladder, making the table for 14 when actually 13 guests are expected, to avoid the unlucky number and that sort of thing. A broken mirror and a black cat crossing the road will make some people uneasy. And do not wish Danes "Good luck" when they are about to gamble or perform – the old "Break a leg" is still preferred.

WORK AND PLAY

Apart from the formal Danish celebrations, you are bound to be invited to more informal gatherings as your network in the country expands. As I warned you in the beginning there are some pitfalls here that you should be aware of. One was the generally very structured format of formal socialising. Another one is, well … informal socialising is pretty structured as well!

At the workplace you should know that in Denmark people distinguish rigidly between work and play. Work is regarded as a serious matter, something that should be completed as fast as possible in a businesslike way so that you can hurry on home. That is how most employees look at it anyway, people who run their own little businesses may have other lifestyles but then they are few in numbers.

I found that out when I started working for the Danish Ornithological Society in Copenhagen after my return, it was my first job for a Danish enterprise. I had been a member of this non-profit organisation since I was a kid and done countless hours of volunteer work. Most of my colleagues were also former volunteers. Nevertheless, as soon as they became employees their attitude changed. Their hobby was now their work, and like them I was expected to fill in time sheets calculating hours at work and participate in lengthy meetings squabbling over work conditions and pay.

During work the Danes do not socialise. There simply isn't the time for it and nobody is interested anyway. The working day is short and cramped with duties and appointments. You don't just drop by to have a friendly chat with somebody at his office unannounced, most likely he will be unavailable and if you somehow force him to take time away from the day's schedule he will be unhappy with the whole thing. It means that he will have to stay at the office late and he will not like that. Try to see it from his point of view – he has kids at the kindergarten to pick up before five o'clock, he also has to do his shopping and cooking before six, in the evening after dinner he may have to mow the lawn and paint the garage, even company directors have to do these things in Denmark!

Therefore, Danish business-people are tough time managers. They don't even like you to call them up on the phone, most requests must be done in writing. You only meet when it is unavoidable and then you sit down right away and get straight to the point, according to some pre-prepared agenda. There is little time for pleasantries and small-talk and deviations and improvisations.

When Danish employees socialise with their fellow workers, however, things are a little different. Now you are off, this is your own time, since this is not work, discussing work is a taboo! Sure, you can gossip about fellow workers and conditions at the office, but you do not talk about any of the business aspects.

This is very different to many other countries I have worked in where people talk about their personal lives at the office and about the business in the evenings. I revisited Singapore shortly after having settled in Denmark and couldn't help marvel at how white collar workers in the MRT underground commuter trains went on and on about their work problems and discussed blueprints and light conductor technology and investment prospects, during their time off! You will never hear such talk in a Danish public transport system.

LET'S NOT DO LUNCH

There is something funny about the Danish lunch-break – it is not really there. Somehow it seems to be missing from society. Sure, the Danes eat at the workplace but they usually bring food with them from home in little lunch-boxes or plastic bags, just like school-children do. Then they sit in a lunch room of some sort within the office or the factory and quickly eat their food, usually open faced sandwiches. Remember that this is not work, so any talk about work is taboo. They flip through the newspaper and then they hurry back to their desks.

Some large companies have catering services that provide fresh food in a canteen in the office-building. But nobody at the workplace goes out for lunch, except maybe business people entertaining clients from out of town. So if you are treated to a Danish business lunch you can be sure that they regard you as somebody special. The Anglo-Saxon tradition of two hour long pub lunches, which are often combined with semiformal business discussions are not a part of the Danish business scene.

I remember my first annual company picnic with the society I work for. We took a ferry across from Copenhagen to Sweden and drove out in a rented bus to look for migratory birds. Incidentally, a gale was blowing and it was continuously pouring with rain, I didn't have a raincoat and got absolutely soaked. Anyway, we stopped for lunch – except there was no lunch. We sat in a canteen in the middle of nowhere (where no food could be bought) and everybody started unwrapping their slightly crushed, old sandwiches. Everybody except I knew that was how it was done. Well, I survived and had a snack on the ferry back later. But just a warning regarding lunch in Denmark – be prepared to bring your own.

An advantage of the Danish system is that offices operate effectively all through the day, there is usually somebody there who can help you. You may get the occasional, "Sorry, but he is out for lunch" message but it is not like some countries, where you might as well forget the idea of contacting anybody between noon and two o'clock.

After work the Danes hurry on home as fast as they can, they have things to do and nobody to help them do it. Don't expect to be invited out for happy hours at the local pub. Certainly working people and even students and young kids lead fairly structured lives; there are volunteer duties, meetings, evening classes, cultural events and sporting practice to fit into the agenda. It all leaves little room for impulsive and improvised socialising.

FOOD INGLORIOUS FOOD

Food is a subjective matter, I am no expert and I have no idea about how to cook myself, so I am in no position to pass judgement but I cannot say that I am personally too impressed with Danish cooking. Considering the amount of time that Danes spend talking about food and writing about it in newspapers and magazines the results are not that impressive. Typically, most quality restaurants in the country are run by foreigners and usually serve French, Italian or Oriental food.

The ingredients in Danish cooking tend to be inferior. The labelling on Danish foodstuffs is very detailed but that does not do much good if the taste is not there. Organically grown food is gaining popularity but according to independent surveys it is not much different from conventional products, except it is on average twice as expensive. Anybody who has tasted vegetables in Africa or beef in South America or fruits in Asia will know that food in the European Union is expensive beyond reason and not particularly good. The exception may be dairy products, berries in season and bread and cakes, but then this again is a somewhat subjective matter.

I must say though, that I love a good, Danish smorgasbord. Different kinds of bread are put on the table, together with an endless variety of fish and meats. Usually you start with raw fish on a dark type of bread made out of rye. The fish is a marinated and chopped herring fillet that comes in four or five different spicy flavours and is truly delicious. Beer and snaps, a 40% proof, terrible tasting liquor, is served. You can drink the beer freely but only drink the first snaps when the initial welcome toast is made by the organisers.

After the meal has been served at a dinner or lunch the real party begins with dancing and party games.

Plates are changed after the fish and you now help yourself to a variety of cut meats, meatballs, pork pate with mushrooms and bacon, fried fish fillet, smoked salmon, shrimps, boiled eggs, tomatoes and other cold foods that you make into open faced sandwiches at your seat. It is a lengthy process and, like the dinner party, it can go on for hours.

Although the smorgasbord is a lunch, it is also supper, no more food will be served that day except a selection of cheese later and coffee and cakes. After that you are free to go but like the formal dinner, there is usually an opportunity to stay on and party and dance until the small hours of the morning.

PARTY GAMES

Usually a lunch type celebration is less formal by nature than the dinner. It is used for pre and after Christmas parties, house warming parties or neighbourhood get togethers. Often it is organised potluck style, so check if you are supposed to bring some food yourself, even if food is provided you usually have to bring your own drink or pay as you consume by dropping five kroner in the jar every time you go to get another beer.

The Danes will always keep in place their unique habit of fixing themselves around a big table. But on more informal occasions sometimes a little game is played to decide seats, like one sex throwing darts against balloons with names of members of the opposite sex in the party. You then sit next to the person whose name you ruptured, who may not be the one you aimed for. Or sometimes the men are blindfolded and select their partners by touch – not a system that appeals to everyone.

Anyway, I guess these little games do help break the ice. After a long lunch meal and an unknown number of beers and snaps, the mood can get quite rowdy. In the old days, company celebrations were notorious for people getting drunk, thereby making fools of themselves and breaking up marriages in the process. In the more sober

1990s these excesses have gone out of style but it is still alright to let your hair down a bit at a luncheon party.

The slapstick taste of some Danes comes into evidence where these party games are concerned. Where we live, we have had parties at the community centre that included some pretty weird games, these were for late at night after all the kids had been put to bed. I have certainly never seen anything like them outside of Denmark. In one game a man was called forward and made to look like a dwarf, with his arms sticking out of a dress like legs. A second person close behind him then had to act as his arms, shaving, dressing and feeding the helpless victim, while the audience bawled out insults and encouragements.

Later on, a selection of men, embarrassingly enough myself included, were lined up while ladies, through a rubber hose stuck through the zipper in our pants, blew up a condom that we held against the other end of the hose. The first couple to burst their condom won. Does it sound amusing? The Danes certainly thought it was on that occasion and cheered and screamed with laughter all the way.

VISITING FRIENDS

At times you will be invited out for a dinner which is not the event-type of occasion we have already described. These more low-key affairs are a good way to develop friendships and many people are more relaxed in these types of settings.

If you are single and meeting another single person, a dinner at a restaurant is a good idea. The whole situation is less complicated if there are people around you and there are no obligations to become too personal about the relationship. That can come later if the dinner is a success. Usually the party doing the inviting is expected to pay, but even if you are the one being invited there is no harm in offering to pay. If several friends go to a restaurant together they will often split the bill between them so it is acceptable to offer to pay for yourself should your initial offer of footing the whole bill be refused. Rather pay too much than too little. In Denmark you do not go out very often so it will never be a big expense for you and being generous will earn you valuable points.

Apart from this, Danes customarily entertain at home. Couples will often invite other couples into their homes, remember that to a middle-class couple their apartment or their house and garden is a lifetime investment and their pride and joy, so they like to make good use of it. Most Danish families eat supper right at 6 p.m. Social dinners are usually put back an hour or two, but not later than that. When you arrive, bring flowers or a bottle of wine and otherwise be yourself – it is hard sometimes in a new place but it is the best strategy in the long run and most Danes will respect you for it.

Once you have settled in and have been invited out yourself you may want to invite people to your home for dinner. This is a simple matter of following the procedures you have observed in other people's homes. Cook yourself if you possibly can, including bread and cakes, the Danes like things to be self made. If you are unsure as to whether your guests eat certain foods, there is no harm in simply asking them. Danes are not afraid of telling you that they would rather eat something else and if they agree at least they know what they are in for.

Practically all Danes drink alcohol, so if you just keep their glasses filled from the time they arrive your guests will probably have a wonderful evening. Make sure that somebody in the party stays sober enough to drive back or check that your guests walk or take a cab home at the end of the evening; driving intoxicated is not only illegal but also dangerous and irresponsible. The legal limit is 0.08 percent alcohol in the blood, usually about two glasses of wine.

SURVIVING CULTURE SHOCK

No matter how much you want to fit into a new place there will be things that shock you, cultural events and experiences that get you down, disappoint you or even offend you. The following quote is extracted from the official Danish Tourist Board information leaflet printed in English in 1993.

> We love our country. It's a free and peaceful country. It's a fresh and wonderful country. It's a happy country. We're not boasting. We're just stating facts. ... See how we live – close to each other, friendly. ... See how we smile.

If you get your first impressions from this colourful production, or one of the countless others that the ministries and the export businesses produce on Denmark every year, then you may be in for a few surprises once you decide to settle and make this happy and wonderfully friendly little country your home.

You go to the post office and your 100 gram airmail letter abroad weighs in at 103 grams. So, the angry lady at the counter asks you to pay the 250 gram rate which is over three dollars more expensive. It happened to me, although I got so annoyed I cut off a strip of the envelope, thereby reducing the weight by four grams. The post officer didn't mind, most Danes enjoy a good fight.

Or your commuter train ticket expires at 15:35 when your scheduled stop is at 15:37, so the ticket controller tells you to get off one stop early and walk the rest of the way, never mind that the train is running late in the first place – what happened to the friendly smile in the brochure you might ask yourself. This also happened to me, and I still haven't got used to the Danish obsession with rules and regulations.

I must say that I do not find the Danes particularly peaceful. I am slowly getting used to it but the chronic antagonisms of society were highly unsettling at first. Pedestrians despise motorists who in turn dislike cyclists, it is obvious every time you walk down the street. Dog owners detest cat owners and vice versa. Hunters hate animal lovers and animal lovers fight meat producers. The rich reject the poor and the poor abhor the rich. It is all some kind of Danish game that is being played, some of it is for fun and at other times it is more bitter and it is often hard to distinguish which is which.

The Danes are shockingly honest and will come right out and tell you if they don't endorse what you look like or what you do. The advantage of course is that in the unlikely event that they should offer you praise, you know that they mean it!

What can you do about it if you are confronted with these situations? Well, no society is perfect, there are shocking elements everywhere you go, the secret is to focus on the opportunities which are also there and make the most of them. Remember that this is their country, they have stayed there a lot longer than you have and you must respect them before you can expect their consideration in return.

And try to review the four classical options for dealing with culture shock:

• **Escape:** Maybe you are better off somewhere else, think this option through. If is does not apply you must forget about it and go on down the list.

• **Confront:** You can fight the Danes, their system and their stupid rules and way of life, you can try to change it all. Maybe it will do you good, maybe it will do the Danes some good! As long as you do not break the law.

• **Encapsulate:** Withdraw, stay with your own kind, stick to your own language and your own culture, have as little as possible to do with the Danes. This is an option preferred by many refugees who are not in Denmark by choice and who are guaranteed material subsistence anyway.

• **Integrate:** Accept the good and the bad, learn to love the place, learn the language, the history, the culture. Further your education, get a job, get a girlfriend or a boyfriend or, as the next chapter of this book suggests, check out the sights of this remarkable country.

— Chapter Ten —

FREE TIME IN DENMARK

OLE MAN RIVER...

In this chapter I will tell you what you can do in Denmark during your free time. I will not be able to give you all the relevant addresses and contact numbers of sporting clubs and museums and theatres and nightclubs that you might want. But I will show you how you can get this information yourself, for free.

In fact, do not waste your money on a general travel guide to Denmark. Travel guides are great for less developed, 'hardship' destinations but in the case of Denmark, a guidebook will not genuinely tell you what the place is like anyway and all the practical information you need is readily available in English from government agencies and tourist information services. How do you think the travel writer researched his book in the first place? So really, this book you are holding now is all you need, the rest we will tell how to find from a primary source – and all absolutely free of charge!

THE DANES WORK HARD AND PLAY HARD

The Danish workforce is the best in the world – that is (almost) official. A Swiss based management institute, IMD, published a survey in 1994 that arrived at that conclusion. By asking a selection of thousands of business leaders around the world, the United States came out as the best place overall to do business, followed by Japan, Singapore, Hong Kong, Germany, Switzerland and Denmark in that order. But when the factor of quality of the workforce was singled out, Denmark came out on the top of the list.

The Danes work really hard and usually th^y know what they are doing. And it is not only during working hours that they toil, they put out during their free time as well. It is as if some collective hyperactivity grips the nation. When the Danes are through cleaning the house, weeding the garden and waxing the car, they go out and buy a summer cottage or a boat and start painting that one, or they attend classes in cooking or karate or scuba-diving or cycle around the country, some industrious Danes even find the time to cycle around the world!

Even if you truly want to assimilate and be like the Danes this pace might be a little too brisk for you. I certainly know what I like to do during my time off – sit on the back porch of the house and look up at the clouds drifting by, or read a story to my kids, often no more than that. But the active nature of the Danes gives you lots of opportunities to join in if you want to. Just remember that during their free time Danes are still Danes, so you have to play by their rules if you want to get along, and everybody plays to win.

FAVOURITE SPORTS

Sports are the number one Danish free time activity. Memberships in sporting federations total more than three million people, young and old. The most popular sports are, in order of active participants: football (soccer), badminton, handball, gymnastics, swimming, shooting and tennis.

Handball is a mainly northern and central European sport that is played indoors as an alternative to football during the winter season and is also played professionally. The Danes are quite good at this and the ladies' national team were 1995 European Champions and World Cup bronze medalists in Atlanta. In 2002 they won the European Championship.

Apart from these sports, Danish participants regularly excel internationally in sailing (several Olympic gold medals in various disciplines), boxing (former European middleweight champion and IBO heavyweight world champion), speedway motor racing (former world champion) and cycling (several Olympic gold medals through the years and a number three in 1995 in the Tour de France). They have a harder time making an impact in athletics and winter sports. Golf is popular on a recreational level, there are no less than 70 courses around the country, but in spite of this, Danish players have never made a significant contribution in international competition.

The Danish soccer team became known worldwide through a gutsy performance in the 1986 World Cup and they crowned a strong spell when they became 1992 European Champions, knocking out much larger nations like Holland and Germany on the way to the top. The team did this through skilful and constructive play and the Danish supporters also won much acclaim for their cheerful and good natured style. It was an astonishing event, especially considering that Denmark had not even qualified for the finals, they joined in the last minute when the former Yugoslavia was expelled from the tournament. Obviously people flooded into the streets of the major cities in Denmark as soon as the final whistle was blown, the winning team members were lauded as national heroes on their return, and it was generally agreed that for a nation of five million to accomplish something like this was truly exceptional. In the 1998 World Cup, Denmark reached the quarter finals, narrowly losing 2-3 to Brazil. The national team qualified again for Euro 2002. In the 2002 World Cup, Denmark knocked out cup-holders France but then lost 0-3 to

The Danish soccer team – 1992 European Cup champions. (Photo: Empics/ Hulton Deutsch)

England at the second stage.

International sporting achievements like these ones go to show that the Danes are a nation of fighters. They might moan and groan endlessly over welfare benefits and whine about their individual rights but most people know how to dig in their heels and pull when it is required. The combative nature of many can find a good outlet in sporting competitions. Involving yourself in sport is not only a great way to meet people, it is an opportunity to see the Danes at their best and learn to appreciate the country.

A Nation of Competitors

Because Danes follow sport closely, it is a major element in many people's lives, providing daily excitement and entertainment. The tabloid papers and the electronic media exploit all the major sporting events heavily and there seems to always be something going on. Like the weather, sports are highly seasonal in Denmark. But don't expect

175

live coverage of the sports to be as snappy and enthusiastic as in other countries. While Danish participants are among the best in the world, Danish television commentators must be among the most boring! For some reason they seem to lack the ability to really open up and become engaged and absorbed in the action.

Also, coverage features almost exclusively Danish participation. If a Danish tennis 'star' is listed 89th in the world ranking, his every move is examined closely by the media, his name will be on every Danish sporting fan's lips, while few would be able to tell you who is actually ranked first, second and third in the world. It took me a while to figure out why Arsenal, Newcastle, Manchester United and some other teams were printed in bold in the result tables for the English premier league in Monday morning papers – it turned out that they each had a Danish player in the team, so these were the teams to watch.

A survey has shown that at least once a month no less than 67% of Danes go for long walks or bicycle rides, 43% have an exercise routine, 16% participate in competitive sports and 28% go to games as spectators. If you do join in, you will see how it is impossible for a group of Danes to just play a little bit and have fun. There must be a purpose to it all – mainly to win or at least to improve. Give some Danes a ball and they will divide into two opposing teams, friends become enemies for an hour and the players swear and curse when the opposition scores, they urge their team-mates on, scold them loudly when they miss the ball and celebrate triumphantly if their team wins.

THE GREAT OUTDOORS

Although I cannot substantiate this from survey results, I think it is safe to state that next to exercise and sports, the great outdoors has the biggest pull on the Danes. The outdoors is really not too great when it comes to it, certainly not as vast and as wild as it is in other places, but nevertheless the Danes just love getting out into nature during their time off.

True to their character they aim to construe a purpose to it all, so they go out into nature to protect it or kill it, or at least study or reconstruct it. There are a quarter of a million organised nature lovers and 90,000 organised hunters. You can become a hunter if you pass the examination and get a hunting licence. You must also own or rent a place to hunt, you must have a gun permit and then you must have a burning desire to kill or maim your fellow living creatures. Shooting a gun and practising on a target is something most people can enjoy, but killing animals is something different.

Most hunting in Denmark is a kind of put and take routine and farmers raise young from popular game birds, like ducks (especially Mallard) and an introduced Asian species, the Ring-necked Pheasant. For many hunters this is really just an excuse for going on long walks across the fields and into the woods with a dog as company. To practise real, big game hunting, serious hunters go abroad. Poland has become a popular destination of late, where there is plenty of widespread forest with dense populations of deer and wild boar.

In spite of this frenzy of activity I have described, I must say that the Danes sometimes do go out into nature just to be there and relax. Look at a park or a beach some July day when the sun shines from a clear blue sky and the temperature creeps above 20°C. The grass or sand surface will be covered with semi-naked, sometimes totally naked, bodies. Suntanning is a serious pastime and in a country where sunshine is seasonal it is hardly surprising. A darker or tanned complexion is regarded as more healthy looking and apparently the message of increased rates of skin cancer due to exposure to the sun has not yet penetrated the public mind. A natural pale exterior is regarded as sickly looking and less attractive in Denmark.

WHERE TO GO

While the Danish outdoors is neat and tidy and much loved by the locals it is not exactly grand. It is difficult to find an alluring spot anywhere in the country that has not also been found by many people before you. If that is acceptable to you the Ministry of Environment and Energy has prepared about 100 suggestions for hikes into public as well as private forests. Some walks are short, only a few kilometres, others are longer. They are described in free leaflets available from most public libraries and from the public information office – *Statens Information* (see the following chapter, "D.I.Y. Denmark"). Some of the leaflets are available in an English edition.

Near Copenhagen there are pockets of nature – in Frederiksberg Have near the zoo, in Utterslev Mose which is a lake and woodlands area northwest of the city centre and on the island of Amager south of the city (where the Kastrup Airport is located). For those who are especially interested in good birdwatching locations, the Danish Ornithological Society has a free English language information leaflet available about the best places to go. Contact them at:

> 138-140 Vesterbrogade,
> 1620 Copenhagen V
> Tel: 3131 4404
> Website: http://www.dot.dk

Beaches and Coastal Areas

The wide-open beaches of the Jutland west coast are truly stunning and a must-see for any resident or visitor to Denmark. During the summer months this area is packed with tourists, especially Germans who seem to take a fancy to exactly this part of Denmark. Perhaps the older ones still remember the time they spent there during the Second World War waiting for an Allied invasion that eventually landed much further south in France. The concrete bunkers are still there, scattered along the beaches. More likely, the tough Germans are just fascinated by this magnificent piece of nature and it is within easy driving distance from their enormous cities. In some places their roomy Mercedes and Audi cars outnumber the Danish license plates nine to one on the parking lots. For some reason quality cars are half price in Germany compared to Denmark so the Danes view this new 'occupation' by their big, rich next door neighbour with a bit of envy and some resentment. But the Deutsch-Marks ring nicely in the cash registers so nobody complains too loudly. About 90% of all Danish summer cottages are rented out to Germans, who are not allowed to own recreational properties in Denmark.

And why just go to the coast during the crowded summer months? The western coastline is just as magnificent during the off season, when huge waves are pounding the desolated shores. It is the closest thing that you will find in Denmark to a true wilderness.

Locally, beaches can be quite polluted and bathing not advisable so check the tourist information office to see which beaches near you are safe for swimming. A Blue Flag label is an EU standard which marks certified clean beaches with visitor's facilities of high rating. Denmark had 139 'Blue' beaches in 1994, check for the nearest one in your area.

When the weather permits the Danes take advantage of the many stretches of coastline in Denmark. Tourists also, mainly from Germany, come here to find a place in the sun. (Photo: Lone Eg Nissen)

Riverside Recreation

Also in the wilderness category, try to rent a canoe on one of the small Danish rivers. You can get a list of suitable rivers and creeks from the Tourist Information Office. About 20 rivers are considered ideal for canoeing, another 30 or so are barely passable, all the major counties have a stream you can check out. Probably the most famous rivers are Skjernåen, Nørreåen and Gudenåen in Jutland and Susåen on Zealand. By prior arrangement it is possible to have the craft delivered somewhere upstream, then you paddle or drift downhill all day and bring in the boat without having to struggle back upstream. If you want to make it an overnight affair make sure you plan for a place to camp in advance, the Danes are very strict on the rules concerning general access and camping on private and public land. Regulations are actually quite liberal – just make sure you are familiar with the details, they cannot be bent! Usually, canoeing is not allowed after dusk and before dawn or too early in the spring (before June 15). Always be prepared to pay for pitching your tent somewhere and in some places even for using the waterway.

If you know the rules and if the weather holds, canoeing can be a wonderful outing but that is about as far as it goes in Denmark, wilderness-wise. However, the mountains of Norway and the endless forests and rivers of Sweden are not that far away and if you like the outdoors you will not be disappointed, if you are prepared to travel a little.

HOW TO GET THERE

Cycling

In Denmark, try to consider seeing the country by bicycle, if you have the energy and stamina and dare brave the unpredictable weather conditions. You can rent a bicycle for less than US$10 a day in most cities and you can also bring your bicycle on many regional trains, if you should change your mind halfway. In Jutland you can travel long distances by bicycle along abandoned railroad tracks, converted to tarred roads which are off-limits to cars. If you combine this mode of transport with a stay in inexpensive but high quality youth hostels, which in Denmark are designed for individuals and families regardless of age, you will have a different but pleasurable Danish vacation – and cheap too.

When bicycling in Denmark the Danish Cyclist Federation will be able to provide you with more information, they can be contacted at:

> Dansk Cyklist Forbund
> Rømersgade 7
> 1362 Copenhagen K.
> Tel: 3332 3121
> Website: http://www.vicykler.dk

Around 3,500 kilometres of country roads suitable for bicycling but also passable by car have been mapped out as especially scenic. This is the so-called Marguerit Route, little signboards with a yellow and white flower mark the full length of this trail through Denmark, which will take you past 1,000 worthwhile sights – according to the tourist information, I haven't counted them myself.

Cycling is one of the most popular recreational pursuits in Denmark. (Photo: Fyn Tour)

On Four Wheels

There is plenty of information available for the motor enthusiast as well. The annual edition of *Motorway* tells you absolutely everything you need to know about driving in Denmark. It includes: information on traffic regulations; what to do in an emergency; camping sites; tourist attractions and hotels on the way; lists of ferry connections, sailing duration and telephone numbers for reservation; plus a full set of road maps.

This 75 page volume with an English summary is available from The Information Service of the Danish Road Directorate (Tel: 3393 3338; Fax: 3315 6335) or from the major tourist information offices. Price? No charge! Other useful contact numbers for motorists include the private organisation FDM, the automobile association, (Tel: 7013 3040; Fax: 4527 0993). If you break down the main rescue company to contact is Falck Vagtcentralcenter (Tel: 7010 2030).

Trains, Planes and Buses

If you are not prepared to ride a bicycle around the country and if you do not drive, there is really just one way of getting to the attraction – you have to rely on the DSB, the Danish, state owned transport company, operating most domestic trains and buses. DSB is a maze of timetables, travel zones and discount rates, I will not even attempt to confuse you with further information. But a travel agent can enlighten you, or better still just call the DSB information direct, all operators speak English. The number is 7013 1415.

There is another way of getting around – you can fly. For a tourist a domestic flight in Denmark is somewhat silly, the DSB Inter-City trains and ferries are extremely comfortable and will take you anywhere in a few hours for one third the price of a plane ticket. But there are discounts available for some age groups and departure times so if you really are in a hurry check SAS (Tel: 3232 2233) or Maersk Air (Tel: 3231 4444) for further information. You can fly into the airports in the following towns, Billund, Bornholm, Esbjerg, Karup, Odense, Sønderborg, Thisted, Vojens, Ålborg and Århus.

Useful Websites:
Road Directorate: http://www.vd.dk
FDM: http://www.fdm.dk
DSB: http://www.dsb.dk
SAS: http://www.scandinavian.dk
Maersk Air: http://www.maersk-air.dk

CULTURAL ACTIVITIES

In Denmark cultural activities are heavily subsidised by the state. From the budget, almost one billion US dollars is allocated to cultural services, a further 750 million dollars go to recreational services. The Royal Theatre in Copenhagen alone received 266 million kroner (US$44 million) in 1994, which means that each ticket sold was subsidised with about US$112. (It's nice to know how much you are saving if you want to catch a performance!) For those who are interested in the finer details of all this there is a brochure available explaining to Danish taxpayers how their money is being spent. Call the Ministry of Cultural Affairs at 3392 3370 for details.

The Royal Theatre is the showcase of Danish drama, ballet and opera but there are more than 100 other theatres around the country. You can ask at the local tourist information service about where to go and what to see.

The average Dane may not be as culturally interested as the expense suggests and if left to the market forces there probably wouldn't be many attractions left. But the state keeps the traditional culture alive for the benefit of the educated elite and the many tourists. There are 285 museums nationwide, big and small. By far the largest and the most visited is the National Museum, their main branch is right between the Central Railway station with Tivoli next to it and the

183

Christiansborg Palace. This is where it is all happening in Copenhagen. Pick up a free map at the big tourist information office right at the northwestern corner of Tivoli and start to stroll, it is all walking distance from here on, and you will have no trouble finding your way around.

While you are at the office ask also for the "Little Big Denmark" brochure. That is the one I quoted from in the previous chapter, so it is heavily tinted with promotional ballyhoo. (That photograph of a smiling chimneysweep is a bit much; I mean, I have certainly never seen a chimneysweep anywhere in Denmark and certainly not a pretty, blonde lady one at that!) Nevertheless, the leaflet does contain some useful information on activities in Denmark. There is, among other things, a list of major national events throughout the year and many are authentic occasions that the Danish people really support.

Festivals

There are a number of festivals around the country each summer and if you really want to meet some Danes (and I mean tens of thousands of Danes) this is where you should go – if you can get a ticket that is. The big music festival which lasted for four days, Woodstock style, at Roskilde in June 1995 was, with 90,000 spectators, the biggest rock festival in Europe that year.

There are similar festivals annually at Ringe, Funen; Skagen, Jutland (mostly folk music) and at Silkeborg, Jutland. There are also Viking festivals each summer (mid June or early July) at Frederikssund, Zealand and Jels, South Jutland where local members of historic groups re-enact the Viking era. The Copenhagen Jazz Festival is a ten-day event in early July which always pulls some big names in Jazz and at Århus there is a yearly festival in early September with scores of concerts, sporting events, drama, exhibitions and plenty of intoxicated young people on the streets.

These music and cultural festivals really get the young Danes in particular going. And by 'young' in Denmark you include most

*The Copenhagen Jazz Festival attracts many of the world's top performers.
(Photo: Danish Tourist Board)*

people up to 35 years of age or so – many students and academics do not settle into a steady job and a proper career until after that age, when people in many other cultures start thinking about retirement! So there is a complicated structure of subcultures and entertainment facilities, clubs and societies that cater to this group.

You will be impressed with the sophisticated nature of Danish culture and at least the diversity. Take the music scene, all styles are available – from the simplest popular sing along tunes to advanced genres like rap, funk, hip-hop, techno remix, jungle remix, ambient and others that I am not quite familiar with. All the big names in American music at one time or another visit Copenhagen on their European tours. The Rolling Stones and Michael Jackson recently performed in Parken, the national football stadium. Nearby in fancy concert halls you can catch the best in the world of classical music and opera. Art exhibitions range from small amateur galleries in a basement somewhere to the top of the line Louisiana Museum north of Copenhagen, which is visited by more than half a million people every year.

Many Danes never make it to the Royal Theatre or the Louisiana Museum. In Jutland I have an adult neighbour who has been to Copenhagen only once. But out in the countryside the summertime is the season for travelling circuses and for local country fairs. My family and I went to such a fun fair recently, with merry-go-rounds, shooting tents, and different kinds of stalls peddling toys and T-shirts, candy and hot-dogs. There was a pet show, an orchestra dressed up as Bavarians entertained and the many beer booths testified to rumours that at night the place would get pretty rowdy. Only Danish popular music was played and all the time we were there I never saw a single foreigner in the crowds. In Denmark like most other places tourists congregate in certain places designed and developed for them. Look out for these little gems on the Danish cultural and festival scenes, the experience can be one of the most rewarding you will have in Denmark.

TOURISM IN DENMARK

Because there are no border checks or records of European nationals coming or going, there are not really any truly accurate statistics on how many tourists visit Denmark each year but it is a lot. However, you are recorded when you check into a hotel or a camping ground and in 1998 more than 29 million people did just that. Or rather that was the number of total nights spent; about 12 million nights at hotels and motels, half of those by foreigners, and about 17 million nights at camping grounds, around 14 million of those by foreign nationals.

The Danes themselves travel abroad quite a lot. This is a very permeable nation with an active and affluent population and a high proportion of foreign trade, so the border crossings are busy places. More than 16 million passengers fly out of Kastrup (http://www.cph.dk) and the other Danish international airports each year. Although the tourists bring about 22 billion kroner into the economy each year, that happens to be offset by the 33 billion kroner that Danish tourists spend abroad.

The thing about tourism this far north is that it is so seasonal. Apart from the bank holidays there are school holidays during one week in winter (February), one in the autumn (October) and the big summer vacation for seven weeks from the end of June until mid August. Most employees have five weeks vacation per year that they usually choose to take sometimes within this period. So in July motorways are cramped with cars and long queues form at ferry crossings. People by the thousands line up for places at the beach or at commercial attractions that are otherwise lying mostly empty and deserted for the rest of the year.

The tourist business and leisure industry is so well developed in Denmark that even if you are a permanent resident there will always be new places that you can go to. I know that there certainly are scores of sights around the country that I have never seen and real quality attractions of a cultural or scientific or entertaining nature that I ought to take my kids around to experience – some day.

187

The Main Attractions

Each year the Danish Tourist Board publishes a list rating the main commercial tourist attractions in Denmark. And just as certain is the winner – Tivoli (http://www.tivoli.dk) in the centre of Copenhagen. In 1998, three million people walked through the turnstiles. Three million people can't be wrong – and they aren't! Tivoli is a must if you are in Denmark, it is much more than just another amusement park. It is a village within the city and there are things to see and do there day and night. Just walking the trails and having a glass of wine at a lake side cafe is a pleasure. If you don't know where to bring your date in Copenhagen, bring him or her to Tivoli and you can be sure that the evening is going to be a success.

Next on the list comes Dyrehavsbakken (http://www.bakken.dk), ten kilometres north of Copenhagen, near the Klampenborg train station. Another amusement park – the oldest in the world according to the P.R. department – which is not quite as classy as Tivoli but still a lot of fun. Combine it with a stroll or a horse drawn wagon ride in the nearby woods for a memorable experience shared by more than two million people every year.

Tivoli – Denmark's leading commercial tourist attraction. (Photo: Danish Tourist Board)

Other million-visits-a-year attractions in Denmark include Legoland (http://www.lego.com/legoland) in Jutland (1.3 million) and the zoo, west of Copenhagen, (1.1 million). After that comes a long list of minor attractions like museums, water sport centres, and smaller zoos around the country. Since these are money spinning ventures, each will have some sort of colourful brochure or advertisements in Tourist Board maps and leaflets. All these can be collected free of charge from the tourist information offices.

CHECKING OUT COPENHAGEN

For the best information regarding Copenhagen get the annual *Wonderful Copenhagen* magazine from the Tourist Information Office when you pick up your city map, it is free. Focusing on the more cultural events there is also a "Wonderful Copenhagen" brochure available from the office.

There is also a 132 page, pocket size *Copenhagen This Week* booklet that they give away at the information office. This one is packed with shopping adverts, especially for Bang & Olufsen electronic products, amber jewellery, knitwear, down quilts and fur coats. I am no expert on shopping but I am sure that any of these establishments will be more than happy to talk to you!

Since I am basically a family and outdoor person, I am also not equipped to guide you through the more tantalising details of Copenhagen's nightlife but *Copenhagen This Week* is. There you will find advertisements for it all from the, presumably, more sophisticated 'Museum Erotica' over quite respectable restaurants and nightclubs, to the sleazy strip joints and escort services. You need a pretty fat wallet if you want to venture into the more arousing nightlife scene, so these places are mostly frequented by successful businessmen, criminal elements and foreigners, few ordinary Danes have the required resources.

The booklet includes complete lists of sporting opportunities, churches, hotels, restaurants, transport details and museums and

189

sights. If you are not sure which sights to go and see consider a sightseeing tour organised by a commercial company. Yes, you guessed it – the Tourist Information Office has a free brochure! The tours start from the City Hall Square right behind the information office. Prices range from 110 kroner for an hour and a half long city tour to 460 kroner for a trip to the Hans Christian Andersen museum in Odense on Funen and 750 kroner for a two-day excursion to Legoland in Jutland.

Personally, I don't recommend people go to the Little Mermaid, although for most people it is required sightseeing material. This small bronze statue commemorating a Hans Christian Andersen fairytale, later taken up by the Walt Disney company, is nothing much to see and it is a bit out of the way in a remote part of the waterfront. A walk in the city can be a more rewarding experience.

The castles are spectacular and still very much a part of contemporary Danish life. I have mentioned Christiansborg already but probably the grandest one is Rosenborg Castle, where the crown jewels are kept. Amalienborg Palace is the home of the Queen and has a spacious square around it. In between the castles, catch a boat from one of the canal piers in this part of Copenhagen and go for a quick city/harbour tour on the water, it is a pleasant way of resting your feet from all that walking.

The museums will not disappoint you. The National Museum (http://www.natmus.min.dk) is mostly historic while the Royal Museum of Fine Arts (http://www.smk.dk) is just that – packed with fine arts. Walk up the Round Tower if you pass by, strolling down the main pedestrian shopping promenade between Kongens Nytorv (translated "The King's New Square") and City Hall. Walk up the City Hall Tower for a view of the city (a guided tour is available at midday) if you feel like some extra exercise.

I can recommend the Tycho Brahe Planetarium (http://www.tycho.dk), where you can also catch an omnimax film, and the Eksperimentarium in Hellerup, north of the city centre. This is a science centre with hands-on exhibits for larger kids, unfortunately most of the instructions are in Danish only. While in Hellerup consider checking out an unusual sight – the United Breweries where Tuborg beer is produced (Carlsberg beer is produced by the same company in the western part of the city). After the tour of the brewery museum free samples of the products are handed out.

SIGHTSEEING AROUND THE COUNTRY

Outside the capital is the Frederiksborg Castle at Hillerød which is magnificent, as well as Kronborg Castle in Helsingør, where you can also pop across to Sweden. Kronborg was the setting of Shakespeare's play *Hamlet*. West of Helsingør around Gilleleje is a fashionable summer residential district for the locals, although the beach is really nothing to write home about. In Roskilde, west of the capital, there is a famous cathedral where Danish kings and queens are buried. South of Zealand on the island of Møn are some truly spectacular limestone cliffs facing the sea to the east.

On Zealand there is also a rather peculiar theme park established by the candy manufacturer, Bon Bon (http://www.bonbon-land.dk). The products of this company are very popular among Danish children and are marketed under sordid names like "gull droppings," "burping duck" and "rich swine." My own kids eat these sweets all the time and the Bon Bon Land, Disney-style theme park illustrates the characters in vivid detail and has joy-rides and other activities. Over 300,000 people pay to visit this centre each year for Danish culture and sophistication – talk about culture shock!

The island of Funen is … well, the birthplace of Hans Christian Andersen, and not really much else. Two museums in the largest town of the island, Odense, celebrate the famous author. Apart from that Funen is a place most Danes just drive through, although I am sure that the local tourist centre could provide you with suggestions of countless things to do and spend your money on. The Egeskov Castle (http://www.egeskov.com) also on Funen is a private home but open

191

When sightseeing in Denmark a highlight is the well preserved castles throughout the country. (Photo: Fyn Tour)

to the public and is well worth a visit. South of Funen is an archipelago of rural islands which are very picturesque and worth a visit for those with time on their hands.

I have already mentioned a number of attraction in Jutland, like Legoland and the west coast beach. In the far north, the village of Skagen is a wonderful spot, the seas meet at Grenen, the most northerly point of continental Denmark. The landscape is stunning here and during spring migration (April–May) Skagen is renowned for its congregations of migratory birds, including many birds of prey and rare species. Later in the summer, people invade the beaches and in the evening the town itself becomes a bustling place with bars and nightclubs jumping along all through the bright summer night. Although Skagen is somewhat special, there are similar villages and camping grounds with the same routine all down the west coast of Jutland and on the islands of Fanø and Rømø to the far south, facing Germany.

The town of Ålborg has a zoo (http://www.aalborg-zoo.dk), an amusement park and an Aqua-land, which is a water activity leisure centre, the biggest in Europe. Århus has no zoo but an amusement park and several historical villages. Within driving distance to the southwest at Givskud there is a drive-through safari park (http://www.givskudzoo.dk). North of Århus is a giant and truly impressive outdoor entertainment centre at Djurs Sommerland (http://www.djurssommerland.dk), open from mid May until late August. You can swim, sail, drive, shoot, play mini-golf and go for rides all day for free once you pay the entrance fee (95 kroner). There are several such centres in Jutland but I have been to this particular one and can recommend it, the kids absolutely loved it.

And need I say it? The tourist information office in Copenhagen and all the major towns have multilingual brochures available for free, detailing all of these attractions. They will explain about all the major sights in the rest of the country in fine detail. Just follow the blue and white signs with a large "i" for Information Office every place you go and you can never go wrong.

Chapter Eleven

D. I. Y. DENMARK

In Denmark people take great pride in the Do-It-Yourself tradition. It is no shame to do all the housework and practical chores yourself; on the contrary, if you are self-reliant and skilful it gives you status. In Denmark knowledge is power, so here is a quick rundown to get you on your way, it is far from all you need to know, but it will help you get started.

GOVERNMENT AND POLITICS

Elections for the 14 counties and 275 municipalities are held every four years. Elections for the 179 member parliament must be held within four years but are often called earlier by the prime minister.

After the November 2001 general elections the following parties were represented:

Name	Platform	Members
Venstre	*Venstre* means left in Danish but the platform is right-wing. Rural/new-right voters	56
Social Democrats	Centre/left. Working middle-class party	52
Danish People's Party	New right-wing, anti-refugees	22
Conservatives	Old right-wing/businessman's party	16
Socialist People's Party (SF)	Socialist, left-wing	12
Radikale Venstre	Liberal right	9
Christian People's Party	Christian values	4
The Unity Party	Red-green, old communists and new anti-globalization voters	4
Greenland	N/A	2
Faroe Islands	N/A	2

The current government is a right-wing minority coalition between Venstre and the Conservatives, commanding 72 seats which means that all legislation must have support from outside the government.

Recent Prime Ministers

- Jens Otto Krag (Social Democrat): 1962–68/1971–72
- Hilmar Baunsgaard (Radikale Venstre): 1968–71
- Anker Jørgensen (Social Democrat): 1972–1973/1975–1982
- Poul Hartling (Venstre): 1973–1975
- Poul Schluter (Conservative): 1982–1993
- Poul Nyrup Rasmussen (Social Democrat): 1993–2001
- Anders Fogh Rasmussen (Venstre): Since 2001

IMPORTANT EVENTS AND CONCEPTS

Some concepts important to the Danes have been covered in other chapters. Here are a few not mentioned which nevertheless form part of the Danish national identity:

Dybbøl Mølle: The scene of a heroic battle at the southern border in 1864 which ended in an honourable retreat (the Germans may have another version of these events). Today it remains a symbol of Danish nationalism.

Andelsbevægelsen: A cooperative marketing system formulated during the 19th century by farmers, something like a union for food producers that Danish development agencies have tried to introduce in the third world.

1968: The year where radical reforms and liberalism peaked. Persons active during this period are even referred to as "1968 ere."

Energy Crisis: In 1973–74; the Arabs cut off oil exports for a while, prices skyrocketed, the world economy nose-dived, Denmark and the western world were never quite the same after this trauma.

Nordisk Fjer: In 1990 a respected family concern by that name went belly-up in a scandal of financial deceit and swindle, including the suicide of the chairman of the board, an event that marked the end of the 'greed-is-good' philosophy of the 1980s.

Janteloven: The Law of Jante; a fictive set of derogatory rules promoting uniformity and mediocrity, a concept always scorned by Danes – but usually adhered to!

Kulturkløften: The Cultural Divide; another fictive concept describing the line between educated admirers of fine art and the general public.

May 18 1993: On the evening of the last referendum finally approving Denmark's commitment to the Maastricht Treaty, the losers (the NO voters) took to the streets and started fighting the riot police, who battled back firing handguns and wounding 11 demonstrators.

The incident has preoccupied the Danish media ever since and the debate over excessive force by the police continues to be a topic for debate all over Denmark.

NAME DROPPING

Some people are, as the saying goes, world-famous in Denmark. Most likely you have never heard of them but they are household names to every man, woman and child in their native country. Some, like current television stars and members of national sporting teams, come and go each year as their popularity and performances peak and fade. Others develop a more permanent status and become engraved within the Danish national identity at least for a decade or a generation. You are not fully integrated until you can nod knowingly when these names pop up in dinner conversations:

The library is a great source of information. In Denmark libraries are well equipped and information is easily accessed. (Photo: Jens Henriksen)

197

Historic Figures

Holger Danske: Mythological warrior believed to have lived around AD750. A statue of him sleeping is in the basement of Kronborg Castle. The legend goes that Holger Danske will wake up and save the nation when it is in peril – which should be any time now!

Nikolai Grundtvig (1783–1872): Poet, clergyman and humanitarian who believed in education for the peasantry, founder of the popular People's High Schools for adult education.

Ludvig Holberg (1684–1754): The Danish Shakespeare, a playwright whose plays are still often performed.

Peter Tordenskjold (1691–1720): Vice-admiral and celebrated maritime war hero who won his everlasting claim to fame by blasting the Swedes on several occasions before he died at a young age in a duel (with a Swedish officer).

Entertainers

Benny Andersen: Writer of many popular songs and stories for children and adults.

Otto Brandenburg: Popular actor and singer who often portrays the typical Danish working-man.

Suzanne Brøgger: In spite of a small literary output, a writer and public speaker often in the news.

Piet Hein: Talented engineer, writer and humanitarian, for many years acclaimed in Denmark and abroad for his designs and poems. His son carries on with the family business.

Poul Henningsen (1894–1967): Industrial designer, writer and a great humanitarian who often aggravated his contemporaries. His famous 'P.H.' lamp hangs over many Danish dinner tables today.

Peter Høeg: A young author whose novels have won him a large audience both in Denmark and abroad, where he has sold millions of copies and been on the New York bestseller list for months.

Robert Jakobsen: Famous and controversial sculptor.

Johannes V. Jensen (1873–1950): Writer, little known today but the only Dane ever to receive the Nobel Prize in literature in 1944.

Asger Jorn (1914–73): Famous and no-longer-quite-so-controversial painter.

Morten Korch (1876–1954): Writer of romantic novels and movie-scripts still in use today.

Kim Larsen: Pop-musician, on stage since the 1960s. Although he flopped when he tried to work in the United States, he is today the ultimate rich and famous Danish entertainer.

The state provides a wealth of information on almost any topic you will need to know about and all free of charge. A great place to start finding out about the country is at the Tourist Information Offices – they are easily located by the large "i" outside the building.

Jørgen Mylius: Famous radio D.J. and television game show host.

Carl Nielsen (1865–1931): Composer whose music is still often played.

Lise Nørgaard: Best-selling author making millions by exhibiting her actually-quite-ordinary life.

Dirch Passer (1926-80): The most famous comedian in Denmark in the last century, his movies are still shown today.

Ulf Pilgaard: Comedian, a more contemporary version of Passer.

Halfdan Rasmussen: Writer of poems and stories for adults and children, often with a humanitarian message.

Klaus Rifbjerg: Bestselling author, now getting on in years.

Shu-bi-dua: By far the best-known Danish pop-group and something of a national institution – although I will bet you have never heard of them; unlike the Swedes, Danish performers do not appeal to an international audience.

Eddie Skoller: Talented singer, comedian and entertainer who also performs in English.

Ove Sprogøe: Famous actor who does both serious and popular parts.

Henrik Voldborg: Television weatherman and tabloid icon.

CULTURAL QUIZ

You will have noticed by now that the Danish people are very particular with regards to the way they do things. A highly organised and regulated society that nevertheless places a strong emphasis on individual freedom, equality and liberalism can certainly take a little getting used to. So, have you got the social skills to make it in Denmark? Try this quiz and find out.

SITUATION ONE

The stewardess on the speed-ferry between two islands approaches you on arrival and tells you sternly to return to your seat and put it back into an upright position. Do you:

A   Tell her to leave you alone and do it herself.

B   Ask for her name so that you can submit a written complaint later to the ferry company about the attitude of the staff.

C   Apologise politely and go back to adjust the seat.

Comments

Most Danes would never end up in this situation in the first place. They would know that service staff do not go beyond the call of duty, which is usually very narrowly defined. It was announced on the P.A. system that passengers are supposed to adjust the seats back before leaving and Danes tolerate no mistakes.

If it did happen to them many Danes would pick option A, although I cannot recommend it, as it would surely create an unpleasant scene.

Forget about B, it would be a total waste of time. You could never report service personnel in Denmark for poor performance, as the local standard is very different from elsewhere and the strong trade unions would support this stewardess all the way.

The best course of action here is to swallow your pride and do as option C suggests.

SITUATION TWO

You are travelling on the ferry with your two pre-schoolers. They keep running across and staring and pointing at this other child who is carrying a huge teddy-bear. Do you:

A   Encourage your kids to go and play with the other child.

B   Move across to the other family so you can chat about your children.

C   Grab your kids and tell them to stop running about, to sit quietly and not stare at strangers.

Comments

Option B is definitely out, most likely the other parent or family would rather be left alone, most Danes resent being crowded or befriended by strangers.

Many Danish parents would opt for C, staring and pointing fingers is considered rude and kids are taught this at an early age.

Since you are a newcomer you might get away with option A, you should be prepared to back out if the other family rejects your kids but then again you might find new friends this way.

SITUATION THREE

At the dinner party the conversation is about law and order. Nine convicted murderers and drug dealers have just escaped from prison and cannot be found. Do you:

A   Proclaim loudly that where you come from these people would never have been in jail in the first place. They would have been hanged – and rightly so!

B   Agree quietly with the general opinion around the table that if the poor criminals had only been given better conditions and more home leave this would never have happened.

C   Change the subject and ask for the chocolate mousse recipe.

Comments

Option A is the sure road to total isolation in Denmark. There are some universal values that the Danes regard as sacred, they cannot be discussed, even if you come from an area where you feel other arrangements work a lot better. These values include the rights of the accused and convicted to humane treatment, freedom of the press, freedom from poverty, welfare for the handicapped, racial equality and a one-man-one-vote type of democracy. You had better memorise this because questioning these rights is absolutely taboo and trying to change people's minds will get you nowhere.

Option B is not recommended, faking a false opinion is not a pleasant experience and you probably cannot keep it up in the long run.

Pick C and get that recipe whether you need it or not!

SITUATION FOUR

Your friends around you start discussing the latest computer software package that has been introduced on the market. Since you did your thesis in just that aspect of software development you feel compelled to join in. Do you:

A   Suppress your ambition to speak up so as not to be seen to be boasting.

B   Enlighten your friends by explaining to them that they have totally misconstrued the entire concept.

C   Propose to do a formal lecture for the whole group at another occasion.

Comments

The Danes like to think that they are instant experts in whatever subject they engage in – since they study and work hard it might actually be the case.

Option A might be a tempting choice in such an intimidating atmosphere but it will get you nowhere in the long run – sure, the Danes dislike bragging but you just have to be prepared to bulldoze your way into society if you want to make it.

If you choose option B be prepared for some resistance, but if you know your stuff your friends will respect you for speaking up.

Option C would be your best bet, if you really have valuable knowledge or skills, present them in a formal way, the Danes love classes and lectures. They will not believe what you tell them in casual conversation but they will believe a book you have written.

SITUATION FIVE

Your income tax return form has been returned with major changes. The tax office estimates that you are hiding income and assets abroad from them and have arbitrarily hit you with a substantial bill for back payments. Do you:

A   Engage a high-powered tax attorney to take the case.

B   Write to the office yourself hoping to sort things out.

C   Quickly pay-up the outstanding tax although it is clearly unreasonable so that you will not get run out of the country.

Comments

Option C is out of the question in Denmark. There is no way that a minor dispute with the tax department or the police will put your immigration status in jeopardy, only felony convictions involving long prison sentences can lead to expulsion.

Option A is not really appropriate, only if you run a business will the advice of an accountant be required.

Most likely you can sort out the matter yourself, there are several avenues available to you. As option B suggests, write to the munici-pality, maybe set up a meeting and appeal to the national court of taxation if necessary. It is a tough and probably annoying process but don't be afraid to stipulate your rights when dealing with the authorities – the Danes will expect it.

SITUATION SIX

You want to meet the head of the department of an office you are dealing with. Do you:

A   Call up this VIP for an appointment.

B   Have a friend introduce you.

C   Write a formal introduction requesting a meeting.

Comments

You can try option A but most likely it is not going to work. Working people with any influence in Denmark are so busy that just catching them on the phone is a difficult thing to do.

The secretary will not help you unless he/she knows who you are and B will not get you far, your personal connections will make little difference.

In the end you have to resort to C. Many doors are open to you in Denmark, you can go and see even CEOs and ministers but only if you are able to put forward a concrete and relevant proposal for the meeting beforehand.

TRIGG

SITUATION SEVEN

Your supervisor at work calls you into his office and tells you bluntly that your latest report was a load of rubbish, produced in the wrong format and packed with errors and inaccuracies. Do you:

A   Tell him you are sorry and that you will do better next time.

B   Ask for a clearer explanation, pointing out exactly what the problem is.

C   Tell him that his supervision has been inadequate and that he ought to do more of this work himself anyway.

Comments

Many Danish employees would choose option C. But obviously this tactic would lead to a dangerous confrontation and it is not recommended for newcomers.

Option B would just lead to more criticism and arguments when the situation has already been clearly explained to you.

Use option A. Your supervisor will be surprised that you do not answer back, but pleasantly so and it will earn you points. You can always find out later by talking to different people at the office how you can perform better next time around.

SITUATION EIGHT

Your Danish assistant has not submitted his work on time and when it finally arrives it is incomplete and imprecise.
Do you:

A   Confront him and tell him that if he doesn't improve you will have to let him go.

B   Go to your own boss and complain about him.

C   Say nothing and do the work yourself.

Comments

Option B might work in some places but it is generally not a good procedure. Being in any way associated with poor performers will always somehow reflect on yourself.

Option A is the standard Danish way of doing things and therefore totally acceptable.

But why not try C? Afterwards spend some time with your assistant, find out why he is not achieving his work targets and how you could help him. It is not the Danish way – but who says that you must be just like the Danes all the time?

SITUATION NINE

You have contracted someone to paint all the woodwork in your new home. You are not happy with the results. Do you:

A   Politely ask the painter to improve in certain spots.

B   Pay him off and do the rest yourself.

C   Confront him, tell him that he is useless and that you will sue him if he doesn't immediately do it all over again.

Comments

Now you are in the driving seat. Option B of course will just have the painter laughing all the way to the bank and will mean that you have wasted your valuable free time doing the work he should have completed in the first place.

Option A is unlikely to produce any results in Denmark, your politeness will just be misinterpreted as weakness and the contractor will not listen to you.

You have to confront him as option C suggests, there is a good chance that he will improve on the job eventually.

SITUATION TEN

You know a fair number of people in Denmark by now, you are about to turn 40 and you want to celebrate with all your friends. Do you:

A   Let the word out that anybody can drop by your home on the day.

B   Arrange for a dinner-party at your local community centre.

C   Invite everybody you know to your favourite restaurant in town.

Comments

Option A is not possible in Denmark. People are so busy that unless they get a formal invitation weeks in advance nobody would turn up on the day and even if they did, they wouldn't know what to do with themselves under such improvised and informal circumstances.

Option C – sure, if you can afford it! Including an open bar the cost might be stupendous and your guests might not even appreciate the restaurant atmosphere. Save this idea for when you want to see one or two people only.

Pick B, this is what Danes do. Prepare laboriously and expect your guests to stay for most of the day and night.

SITUATION ELEVEN

You are infatuated by a beautiful girl at your new Danish workplace. Do you:

A   Tell her she is pretty and give her flowers and candy at the office.

B   Lure her into the storeroom and embrace her.

C   Try to speak to her when you get the chance and ask her out only when you are sure that the feelings are mutual.

Comments

Option A is a bit risky, you might find yourself accused of sexual harassment and facing all sorts of trouble.

Option B is surely unacceptable, it might work in some countries but in Denmark you would end up under police investigation if you pulled something like that. The general attitude towards women in many jobs can be rather crude, especially in male dominated blue-collar environments but this is supposed to be a light-hearted jargon without any real substance, however offensive it may be.

If you are serious about someone, your best bet is option C. From there you can gradually progress to A but make sure there is reciprocity and try to limit activities around the workplace, where people are generally expected to do just one thing – work!

DO'S AND DON'TS APPENDIX

DO

- Make an appointment before you visit... anybody!
- Find out what your rights are and fight for them.
- Be on time, never late and not too early.
- Take advantage of the many green areas and nature reserves open to the public.
- Get a sweater, a raincoat and a pair of rubber boots and get out there, if you wait for the weather to clear you will be stuck indoors forever.
- Become a member of a society that suits your interests... whatever your interests are, there will be such a group!
- Impose yourself at the work place, show them what you have got.
- Get a tool kit and learn to manage repairs and small maintenance jobs around the house yourself.
- Insist on a written contract is you make an agreement with someone.
- Take advantage of the many formal learning opportunities available during the long winter season.
- Remember to say 'Have a nice weekend... (*Go' veekend...*)' on Friday afternoons, everyone else does.

DON'T

- Talk to strangers, unless you are pretty thick-skinned and ready for a possible rude response.
- Show fear in a hostile or threatening situation, Danes don't respect wimps.

- Be afraid to engage in an argument in public or in the workplace.
- Expect rules to be bended due to your special circumstances, this won't happen.
- Lecture about how you used to do things back home, the Danes are not interested.
- Use the zebra crossing unless the road is clear.
- Go shopping after 6 pm, it simply cannot be done.
- Give money as gifts.
- Ever... ever!... say that you favour the death penalty.
- Brag, if you advertise skills you must be able to back them up... remember, you are dealing with the best workforce in the world (see page 173)!
- Expect to ever be one of them, be yourself.

RESOURCE GUIDE

HEALTH

Righospitalet Blegdamsvej 9 2100 Copenhagen Ø Tel: 3545 3545 Website: http://www.rigshospitalet.dk. **International Health Insurance Danmark A/S** Palægade 8 1261 Copenhagen K Tel: 3315 3099 Website: http://www.ihi.dk.

HOME & FAMILY

Ministry of Education Frederiksholm Kanal 21-25 1220 Copenhagen K Tel: 3392 5000 Website: http://www.uvm.dk. **Danmarks Naturfredningsforening** (Nature Conservation Society) Masnedø Gade 20 100 Copenhagen Ø Tel: 3917 4000 Fax: 3917 4141 Website: http://www.dn.dk.

MANAGING YOUR MONEY
Currency

1 Danish Krone (sometimes translated to Crowns) divided into 100 øre (or ears). Abbreviation is Kr. locally, DKK internationally. Smallest nomination in circulation is 25 øre. Exchange rates obviously vary, in this book the exchange rate DKK6.00 to $US1.00 is used, check the daily paper if you need to recalculate. Credit cards are accepted in most hotels, restaurants and larger shops but not by DSB, the national railroad, bus and ferry network.

ENTERTAINMENT & LEISURE
Shopping Hours

During weekdays shops open from 10:00 a.m. to 6.00 p.m., some supermarkets until 8:00 p.m. On Friday opening hours are extended for one or two hours. Banks open from 9:30 a.m. to 4:00 p.m. weekdays, and until 6:00 p.m. Thursday and are closed on weekends.

The post office opens on weekdays from 10:00 a.m. to 5:00 p.m. (but in larger towns from 9:00 a.m.) and on Saturday from 10:00 a.m. to 12:00 p.m.

If you are a tourist you can reclaim the Value Added Tax (*MOMS* in Danish) for larger purchases on departure, check at the store for procedures.

Tipping

Generally tipping is not expected, even by waitresses or taxi-drivers. However, it is not refused so feel free to round up the bill or tip for service above and beyond the call of duty.

TRANSPORT & COMMUNICATIONS
Taxis

In Denmark you usually call for taxis and there is no extra charge for this. In Copenhagen and some major towns taxis can also be flagged down on the streets. The meter drop rate is DKK16 between 6:00 a.m. and 6:00 p.m. (otherwise DKK22) with DKK7.65 added per kilometre moved or DKK3.75 per minute. The taxi will take your bicycle along for an extra DKK10 surcharge.

Driving

Foreigners can drive in Denmark on their native driver's license as long as they remain on tourist status. Police advise foreigners from countries using a non-European alphabet to acquire an international license. No later than two weeks after obtaining resident status the foreigner must convert the license to Danish. Citizens from within the EU have been exempted from this rule since 1 July 1997.

Speed limits are 50 kph in towns, 80 kph on country roads and 110 kph on motorways. At junctions watch the signs, if two equally important roads meet up, give way to motorists on your right. The legal blood alcohol limit is 0.08% (about two beers), this rule is strictly enforced. Seat belts must be worn by everybody in the car.

Headlights must be on at all times when driving. Motorcyclists must wear helmets, even many cyclists do, although it is not compulsory.

Remember to set the plastic clock (parking disc) in the car windscreen when you park on a street where a large white 'P' on a blue background is displayed and be back within the allocated time printed on the sign. In most large parking lots you buy a ticket from a vending machine.

Car Rental

Car rental is a bit steep, starting at DKK350 per day for the smallest models, and is often quoted with limited mileage. Check the yellow-pages and call around for the best quote, these people all speak English. Note that prices are lower if you are not a Danish resident, foreigners can travel on tax-free plates.

Petrol Prices

Petrol/gasoline is currently DKK8.35 per litre for premium unleaded, which is similar to Germany and other continental European countries (except Norway which is a major oil exporter but has by far the highest petrol prices in the world!). Diesel is cheaper at DKK7.31 per litre but both prices are scheduled for gradual increases in future years as a new set of environmental tariffs are about to be implemented.

Using the Telephone

The best way of making contact in any place is by using the telephone and Denmark is no exception. Most people answering phones will be able to help you out in English. Check the first few pages in the directory for further information and the yellow pages for things you need. Let your finger do the walking as the cliche goes – it really works. One call may not do it, I have sometimes had to speak to five or six different people to get the information I needed but in general, information in Denmark is readily available and easy to get at. If you cannot find it in the book just dial **118** to get local telephone information or **113** for other countries. Be aware, however, that it costs eight kroner, which is almost a dollar and a half every time you connect up to information, so it can quickly add up.

In an emergency dial **112**, for connection to the relevant department. If you call abroad just dial **00** (international) + the country code + the number you wish to dial. Calling the UK, for example, is thus: 00 + 44 + area code + number.

GENERAL COUNTRY INFORMATION
Electricity
220 volt AC in 50 cycles. Only high-current sockets in kitchen and utility rooms are grounded. Television frequencies are compatible to European/Asian systems.

Measurements
Strictly metric, few Danes are familiar with inches and gallons and Fahrenheit degrees. If you are unfamiliar with metric measures, conversion charts are easily available.

General & tourist advice bureaus & websites
Wonderful Copenhagen Tourist Information 1 Bernstoffsgade DK - 1577 Copenhagen V Tel: 3311 1325 Website: http:// www.woco.dk.

Immigration, residency & nationality issues
Statens Information Nørre Farimagsgade 65 1364 Copenhagen K Tel: 3337 9200 Fax: 3337 9299 Website: http://www.si.dk. **Department for Aliens** Ryesgade 53 2100 Copenhagen Ø Tel: 3536 6600 Fax: 3536 5420 Website: http://www.udlst.dk. **Danish Refugee Council** Borgergade 10.3 Sal 1300 Copenhagen K Tel: 3373 5000 Website: http://www.drc.dk. **Ministry of Foreign Affairs** Asiatisk Plads 2 1448 Copenhagen K Tel: 3392 0000 Fax: 3154 0533 Website: http://www.um.dk

Ministry of the Interior Christiansborg Slotsplads 1 1218 Copenhagen K Tel: 3392 3380 Website: http://www.inm.dk.

Country statistics

Size 43,000 square kilometres (16,630 square miles) not including Greenland and the Faroe Islands. **Population** 5.2 million people; Copenhagen (greater area): 1.2 million, Copenhagen (city district only): 467,000, Århus: 275,000, Odense: 182,000, Ålborg: 158,000, Esbjerg: 83,000.

BUSINESS INFORMATION
Legal Aid

A service available in many bigger towns is free legal aid. I used this service myself once when I was uncertain about some copyright matter and didn't really feel I had to trouble a professional law firm with it. Check in your local municipality to see if there is such a service in your area. The nearest public library is another good source of information on this and other services available to the public.

USEFUL WEBSITES

www.jubii.com http://www.danmark.dk http://www.dst.dk www.denmark.dk http://www.copenhagenpictures.dk http:// www.turisten.dk

FURTHER READING

There is plenty of literature available on Denmark. Some are pretty coffee table books introducing Denmark as the fairytale land of endless sunshine falling across green fields and neat farmhouses with happily smiling people on the porch waving invitingly to the visitor.

Others are dry, government-supported publications, presenting would-be immigrants and scholars with the necessary facts.

In Danish, there is a third category of books aimed at social criticism. Usually illustrated with grim black and white photographs of lonely old people, neglected children and squatters fighting the police in the slums, these books reflect the Danish preoccupation with welfare and humanitarianism.

Here is a list of some of the most useful English language references currently available:

General Guides and Coffee Table Books

Aistrup, I. *Denmark*, (2nd. edition) Høst 1995. A lot of colourful photos showing the country through the seasons. 74 pages.

Himmelstrup, P. *Discover Denmark*, The Danish Cultural Institute, 1992. A detailed, heavy-going account of Danish life, especially regarding culture and art. 240 pages.

Nye, D. E. *Denmark and the Danes*, Danish Society for the Advancement of Business Education, 1992. Useful introduction written by a foreigner, especially for young students. 40 pages.

Taylor-Wilkie, D. (ed.) *Denmark*, APA Insight Guides, 1993. A comprehensive guide in high quality APA format. 344 pages.

Travelling

You can save your money by accessing the Tourist Information Service. It has a wide range of advertisement leaflets and maps freely available.

Bed and Breakfast, a Guide to Farm Holidays and B&B in Denmark, 1994.

Camping Denmark Yearbook.

Immigration Information

If you decide to stay on check out Statens Information for official instructions or get:

Davidsen, L. (ed.) *Welcome to Denmark*, Dansk Flygtningehjaelp (Danish Refugee Council) 1984. A no-frills production, mostly targeted at political refugees. 126 pages.

Vedel, P. V. (ed.) *Hello Denmark*, Stout, 1993. A handy government supported guide for long term visitors. 176 pages.

History and Politics

Kjersgaard, E. *The History of Denmark*, Ministry of Cultural Affairs, 1990.

Danish Political Parties – In Their Own Words, 1994. Ministry of Foreign Affairs, 24 pages.

Culture and Society

Andersen, H. C. *Eighty Fairy Tales*, Hans Reitzel Publishing, 1994. 483 pages.

Cave, W. & Himmelstrup, P. *The Welfare Society in Transition*, Danish Cultural Institute, 1995. 232 pages.

From the Ministry of Education:

Adult Education in Denmark, 1993.

Education in Denmark: A Brief Outline, 1992.

The Education System, New Edition 1995.

Danish Film – Through the Years, Danish Film Institute, 1990.

Literature from Denmark, Danish Literature Information Centre, 1991. Especially covering quality Danish literature available in English.

Reddy, G. Prakash, *Danes Are Like That*, Grevas, 1993. An Indian anthropologist's impressions of life in a small Danish village. 175 pages.

Business

Business Denmark Yearbook, Federation of Danish Industries.
Direct Taxation in Denmark, New Edition, Inland Revenue Department, 1992. 68 pages.
The Danish Economy, Ministry of Finance, 1993. 23 pages.

Language

Danish for Travellers, Berlitz Guides, 1989. 192 pages plus cassette.
White, J. R. *Danish Made Easy*, Høst, 1978. Some everyday phrases and general information. 63 pages.
Woodbridge, H. *Danish in Three Months*, Hugo, 1992. Four cassettes, book 189 pages.

Other Sources

Some of the organisations listed in the last chapter, like the Foreign Ministry, the Tourist Information and the Danish Refugee Council have their own publications and leaflets in the English language, as well as in German, French, Spanish, Arabic, Turkish, Polish, Vietnamese, Tamil and others.

For those who pick up Danish there is obviously so much more information available. As a starter I will recommend *Facta Danmark*, a new edition is published at the end of every year by Systime Publishing. It contains a lot of useful information in concise form.

For this book I also made extensive use of governmental data released through: Statens Information, Dansk Turistraad, Nordisk Raad, Kommunernes Landsforening, Danmarks Statistik and various ministries. For the revised 2003 edition, I surfed the website, **http://www.jubii.dk**, for electronic updates.

THE AUTHOR

Morten Strange was born in Copenhagen, Denmark in 1952. He studied economics at the University of Aarhus in Jutland. In 1973, he moved abroad to work in the offshore oil business, living in Norway, Scotland and England. He served as a sergeant in the Danish army from 1975 to 1977. In 1980 Morten and his wife moved to Singapore, where he worked as a petroleum engineer travelling to Malaysia, Indonesia, the Philippines, Thailand, Hong Kong, China, Japan  and the United States on assignments. In 1986 he retired from the oil business and started his own company, Flying Colours, photographing and writing about nature and birds in the Southeast Asian region for books and magazines in Asia and the English-speaking world.

In 1993 Morten and his family moved back to Denmark, where he continued his writing and photography career. In 1999, the "culture shock!" got too much for Morten, and he returned to Singapore where he now has a new career marketing nature books for Nature's Niche Pte. Ltd. In 2002 he married a Singaporean Chinese and they now have a beautiful little baby boy.

Morten has published books about Danish birds, oil well drilling in the North Sea and travelling in Alaska. He is also the author of a number of photographic guides to birds in Southeast Asia and East Africa, see **www.naturesniche.com** for more details.

INDEX